JOHN STEINBECK

A STUDY OF HIS FICTIONAL WOMEN

Dr. (Ms.) Sushma Arya

SHIPRA

ISBN 81-7541-042-6
First Published in India in 1999

Published by
SHIPRA PUBLICATIONS
115A, Vikas Marg, Shakarpur,
Delhi-110092 (India)
Phones.: 2458662, 2423078
Fax: 091-11-2458662, 2423078
Email : siprapub@satyam.net.in

Laser Typeset by
IDRI's Business World
Delhi-110 092

Printed at
Nice Printing Press
Delhi

Dedicated

to

My Most Revered Father

Foreword

Ms. Sushma Arya's study of women in the fiction of John Steinbeck is decidedly an important critical work. Compared to the similar studies made by the Indian scholars, it can be considered outstanding. Analysing the entire range of long and short fictional compositions of the American novelist, Ms. Arya has offered a comprehensive view of the variety of female characters, covering their familial, societal and, above all, genderic status in the industrial civilization of the West.

Since the study of American literature in the Indian Universities was introduced under the direct sponsorship of the United States Information Service through its academic agencies called United States Educational Foundation in India and the American Studies Research Centre, John Steinbeck has not been an inevitable choice in the American Literature course of the Departments of English as has been the case with authors like Hawthorne, James and Hemingway, or Whitman, Dickinson and Frost. The official underplaying of Steinbeck by the USIS is understandable, and so is the Indian clientale's adherence to the official line. Although the USIS withdrew its patronage to literature studies long ago, the official prescription of authors to be studied continues to have its hold on the Departments of

English in our universities. Notwithstanding the university courses in American literature, however, John Steinbeck continues to remain one of the major writers of fiction America has produced, comparable to the European giants like Tolstoy and Dostoevsky. His place in the history of modern American fiction between the two World Wars remains secure and unchallenged. His importance as novelist lies in his being the most representative writer of the period as also the most comprehensive and critical.

The importance of Ms. Arya's critical study of the female characters in the novels and stories of John Steinbeck lies in its disinterested examination of the artworks as in themselves they really are. Resisting the temptations of fashionable critical ideologies, such as Marxism and Feminism, historicism and psychologism, she has kept her vision clear, uncoloured by any of the postmodernist critical theories. She has viewed the status of women in the American society between the wars as it is depicted by the great novelist. Ms. Arya's work shows a sensitive mind at work, bringing to bear upon the subject of study an intensive investigation and sharp perception. Its being free from the cliched critical jargons, which conceal more than what they reveal, makes its reading a pleasant and rewarding experience.

In sticking with full strictness to her critical credo of making an honest assessment of what is actually there in the constructed plots of the novels and short stories, Ms. Arya comes out with both the strong and weak points of John Steinbeck as a writer. Note, for instance, the following as a part of the conclusion to the critical investigation;

> Steinbeck's writings reflect his social, cultural, historical and personal limitations where women are concerned, although in the matters of sexuality he was a pioneer in

> overcoming taboos about what it was permissible to portray. For instance, *The Grapes of Wrath* was banned from high school libraries for its alleged 'vulgarity', and it was called 'a morbid, filthy worded novel'? But in portrayal of women Steinbeck remains traditional, and he assigns his women the traditional female occupations such as mothering, teaching school children, and prostitution.

Thus, in her unbiased study of an important aspect of Steinbeck's fiction, Ms. Arya does not limit the scope of her work by dealing with isolated female characters in the various works. Instead, she always makes an integrated examination of the whole work of which the female characters are a part. Always placing these characters in their respective fictional contexts, she seldom misses the manifold significance of any individual female in Steinbeck's fiction. As a result, the women in different plots defy the stereotype mythical descriptions made by the critics belonging to different schools.

Ms. Arya not only offers analysis of various fictional works of Steinbeck but also views the author in the overall perspective of the American novel as it has come down from Hawthorne to Hemingway. Thus, one can find in this major critical work on Steinbeck not only a detailed study of the female characters but also an overview of the fictional world of the author as well as his place in the history of the American novel. Convincingly documented with citations from the texts of the artworks Ms. Arya's study is a valuable one, which offers insightful readings of the various works and makes thought-provoking remarks about the author's limitations as an artist.

At a time when the postmodernist theory has termed the traditional aesthetico-moral concerns of literary criticism as outdated, no longer relevant to the present-day world, and has converted the business of criticism into cultural studies, bringing to the fore the repressed and marginalised voices, the importance of a writer like John Steinbeck is bound to increase. His novels and short stories, with their wealth of social details and political overtones, offer to the postmodernists a fertile ground for socio-political interpretations. The sheer vastness of his social canvas and the solidity of his social representation are enough to engage for long the present-day scholars of cultural studies. His strength as a novelist sqarely rests on his capturing the historical scene of the 30's and 40's in all its complexity of economico-political structures governing the American society of the time. It goes to the credit of Ms. Arya that despite the severe limitations of her topic, which focuses on the status of women in steinbeck, she has been able to bring out the cross-currents of socio-economic forces shaping and driving the female characters. The success of her study lies in relating the female characters in Steinbeck's fictional world to the various socio-political strands that govern the social structure in which these characters are placed. One may not agree with her on all the points she makes in her study, but one cannot ignore the relevance of her questionings and conclusions to an understanding of the American writer's work. The students and teachers of modern American novel should find Ms. Arya's study a rewarding reading, useful as it is both as an introduction to Steinbeck's work for the beginner as well as a scholarly investigation into a set of pertinent issues related to the status of women in the American society between the two World Wars. Given the vast potential of Steinbeck's narratives and the deep insight of Ms. Arya's interpretations of those narratives, the book, I am sure, is bound to make a place for itself in the inevitable list of reading for the students and scholars of the American novelist. In our time, when there is an unprecedented awakening among women for seeking gender justice and equal status, Ms. Arya's book acquires an added significance. Those looking for the status of women in America in the 30's and 40's can find a useful work in Ms. Arya's study of Steinbeck from the viewpoint of women's status in a man-made world. Hopefully, this would encourage further investigations of this and similar representations in the works of the writers of Steinbeck's hue.

Bhim S. Dahiya

Former Vice-Chancellor
Kurukshetra University
Kurukshetra

Acknowledgements

In the preparation of this work I have been lucky to receive valuable help and guidance from several persons and institutions. First of all, I must acknowledge my indebtedness to Dr. (Ms) Kamlesh Bhandari but for whose unstinted help and wise and systematic guidance from time to time on the study, it would have been almost impossible for me to complete the study. I am also thankful to my mother whose constant presence by my side has been a source of great strength to me. Above all, I owe the completion of this study to the sacred memory of my most revered father who all my life has been a source of great inspiration to me and whose affectionate reminders during his life-time always worked as a pressure to go ahead. My thanks are also due to my friends and relatives for their best wishes and blessings.

I would be lacking in my duty if I fail to acknowledge my gratitude to the authorities at ASRC for not only providing me with necessary books and generals but also for their kind and generous behaviour.

Finally, I wish to thank Mr. J.S. Jagdev who completed the typing job with great care and interest.

Sushma Arya

D.A.V. College for Girls
Yamuna Nagar

Contents

I

Steinbeck and His Critics

It is only natural that a novelist of the stature of John Steinbeck has been exposed to an expansive and wide criticism. Over the past seven decades a large number of reviewers has reviewed and scrutinized his work from various angles. During this long period of critical assessment, the novelist has been both hailed and assailed for the different constituents of his art and craft. More than any other constituent of his work, however, it is Steinbeck's art of characterization which has attracted most diverse interpretations. Critics have made very different interpretations of the large variety of characters the novelist has left behind in his fictional creations. While the critics like Maurice Sands, John S. Kennedy, and Lawrence William Jones, describe his characters as unreal and "types" and also show the novelist's inability in producing life-like characters, those like Gray James, Lester Jay Marks, and Howard Levant characterize them as life-like and "believable" and emphasize "Steinbeck's brilliance in the creation of memorable characters."[1] A close study of the Steinbeck criticism, however, makes one feel that the critical response to his characters in most cases is rather sketchy and has principally stayed with the early descriptions of these characters being wooden and "animal-like".[2]

When characterization itself has not been given a fair deal by the Steinbeck critics, it is only to be expected that they would dwell much less on the women figures in his novels. Even when some of the critics in the late sixties and the seventies turned to his women, they focussed mostly upon his women in the short stories. As for Steinbeck's female characters in the novels, they have either been entirely ignored or have not been given adequate attention. They have been characterized as mere "myths" and "symbols." The reason for these unfavourable descriptions of the women characters is that the critics have approached Steinbeck's fiction with readymade ideational structure of a myth or philosophy. The imposition of an external framework of any non-literary schematism does not permit a critic to see these characters as they really are in the fictional world of the novelist. In order to do justice to the women characters of Steinbeck we shall have to formulate an approach which is not actuated by any prefabricated extra-literary considerations and which directly addresses itself to the fictional constructs of the novelist. Before making clear the direction of this new approach, however, it would be relevant to retrace in brief the history of Steinbeck criticism as it has responded to his characters in general and to his women in particular.

The seminal Steinbeck criticism can be said to have started in the nineteen thirties. The decade predominantly highlighted the reformative aspect of John Steinbeck. Robert Bennet and Claud E. Jones described him as an American novelist working within the native tradition of the "reform" novel. Critics like Burton Rascoe, Samuel Levenson, and V.F. Calverton accentuated his involvement with the problem of good and evil and stressed his unyielding faith in the goodness of mankind.

Thus, these critics laid the foundation for one of the major critical approaches to Steinbeck—that is, they projected his image of a social reformer, an image that stuck to him and continued through the forties. Furthermore, Edmund C. Richard, T.K. Whipple, and Frederick I. Carpenter underlined Steinbeck's versatility. These critics cared to pay little attention to the novelist's art of characterization. Regarding women, only very few collateral critical remarks are available and those too in a negative tone. Edmund Richard represents his contemporaries when he describes Steinbeck as a "masculine" writer and asserts that the Women in Steinbeck is always a destructive force. Surprisingly, even a full-length study like *The Novels of John Steinbeck : A First Critical Study* completely overlooks the aspect of characterization.

In the forties Steinbeck's recognition as a social reformer was further enhanced by critics like Joseph Warren Beach, Alfred Kazin, Lincoln R. Gibbs, Carey McWilliams, Edwin Berry Burgum, and Leo Gurko. These critics found him a writer with a social consciousness whose prime concern is to depict social crises of his times, a critic of social institutions, a reflector of the contemporary American life, a writer who is realistically dealing with the continuing problems of the American life like the labour problem, etc. A more significant development during the decade, however, was the breaking of new grounds in the exploration of the novelist's work. While Barker Fairley[3] appreciated his use of "myth and symbolism," Woodburn O.Ross[4] emphasized his literary kinship with the naturalists and in another essay on the novelist, along with Michael F. Moloney,[5] called him an "irrationalist." Then, there appeared an unfavourable approach to his work spearheaded by critics like Maxwell Geismer, Freeman Champney, Donald Weeks, George

D. Snell and Blake Nevious, who indicted him for his "Gross-sentimentality" accusing him of the over-sentimentalized projection of his characters. However, the most influential critical piece of the decade which acted almost as a trend setter for the subsequent Steinbeck criticism was Edmund Wilson's "*The Californians : Storm and Steinbeck.*" Wilson calls Steinbeck a "biologist" who instead of raising animals to the stature of human beings "assimilates the human beings to animals."[6] In 1942, Alfred Kazin[7] echoes the same viewpoint and declares that Steinbeck's basic and foremost interest is in the animal nature of human life. Later, the same viewpoint is upheld by critics like Freeman Champney, Edmund Magney Claude and Frederick Bracher. Curiously, all these critics are victims of what psychologists refer to as "set". Thus, while Steinbeck's characters do receive attention (though rather unfavourable) in the criticism of the 40s, his women still fail to engage the attention of the critics.

Peter Lisca's *The Wide World of John Steinbeck* and E.W. Tedlock's and C.V. Wicker's *Steinbeck and His Critics*, published in the fifties, instituted a new trend in the criticism of Steinbeck's characters. The latter work in consequential in that it summarizes the major criticism of the 30s, 40s and 50s by concluding that "critics have made serious blunders" in judging Steinbeck as an artist. These writers express the hope that in future "critics will find him to be an artist with an artist's intentions, methods and stature."[8] Perhaps an exception to the category of critics reprimanded by Tedlock and Wicker, Charles Poore[9] appreciates Steinbeck for his skill and efficiency in creating real characters. More important than even Poore's drawing of our attention to the writer's skill in characterization is Peter Lisca's almost singular attempt in inviting our attention to the importance of women in the works of Steinbeck. Contesting the charge that there is no place for women in Steinbeck fiction he asserts: "In the world of his fiction women do have a place, but they seem compelled to choose between home making and whoredom, ...[10] Though Lisca's categorization is not very convincing, still his contribution is significant in that he is perhaps the first critic in the three decades who paid some attention to the women of Steinbeck. Most other critics produced only a pale repetition of what had already been said during the thirties and forties. For instance, John S. Kennedy echoes Edmund Wilson when he attributes to Steinbeck "animalization of characters." Like Maurice Sands he finds the novelist incapable of producing life-like characters; he finds the characters "heavily documented types."[11] The same year Frederick J. Hoffman finds Steinbeck a "novelist of animality,"[12] which charge is later repeated by Walter Fuller Taylor in 1959.

The nineteen sixties was a prolific decade in Steinbeck criticism. Seven full-length studies of Steinbeck's works and scores of short studies came out during the decade. Excepting Richard O'Connor's *John Steinbeck*,[13] which is a biographical study, all other books of the decade are primarily and centrally concerned with the study of various themes in Steinbeck's novels. Regarding characters, the decade is not very conducive, yet one positive feature seen here is that whereas the earlier critics had been completely ignoring his women in the analysis of his fictional constructs, the critics of the sixties pay special attention to the characters and the women, too, receive adequate attention. The critics of the decade can be divided into five groups : one, Lester Jay Marks,[14] Daniel R.Brown,[15] and Peter Lisca,[16] the critics who have censured the characters of Steinbeck; two, the critics like Warren French,[17] and F.W. Watt[18] who in their respective books talk of Steinbeck's particular women; three, Mordecai Marcus,[19] William R. Osborne,[20] and Elizabeth E. McMahan,[21] the critics who have taken up his individual women like Elisa Allen as their subject of discussion; four, the group of critics[22] who are merely repetitive; and, last of all, the critics whose attention has been aroused by the women of the novelist. Joseph Fontenrose quotes Magney's classification of the novelist's women as: (a) women as sexual objects, (b) and motherly figures nearly sexless.[23] Tetsumaro Hayashi finds two types of women in Steinbeck: (a) the women who are the principle of continuity and (b) the women who are the principle of destruction and discontinuity.[24] And Lisca observes the merciful treatment of the author for married women.[25]

The nineteen seventies has been the most productive decade in Steinbeck criticism: more than a dozen books, excluding the biographical ones and the critical anthologies, were published. Farthermost views have been expressed about the novelist's art of characterization. For instance, whereas the critics like Paul McCarthy,[26] Richard Peterson[27] and Sunita Jain[28] react positively to his art of characterization, those like Reloy Garcia,[29] Lawrence William Jones[30] and Roy S. Simmonds[31] find the novelist an utter failure in the matters of his characters; the former group finds his characters "round" and "believable" the latter finds them "flat" and faceless "types." One significant development of the decade is the appearance of a number of articles entirely devoted to the study of women in Steinbeck's fiction. Saikichi Nakashima's[32] "*Steinbeck's Women*" stresses the novelist's failure to portray diverse types of women and attributes this to the limited role of motherhood which is invariably assigned to them. The only other category of women appearing in Steinbeck is, says Saikichi, of childless mysterious women. Sandra Beatty[33] is perhaps the first critic to assert that there are many dynamic and memorable female characters in Steinbeck "who demand and merit close study and critical attention." In her view, the novelist chiefly assigns two roles to his women: they are either wives or mothers. Marilyn Mitchell's[34] "*Steinbeck's Strong Women: Feminine Identity in the Short Stories,*" shows that John Steinbeck and D.H. Lawrence are the only novelists of the time "Who tried to release Women from the pasteboard, shadowy role she generally assumed in fiction." Another critic of Steinbeck's women, Mimi Reisel Gladstein asserts that "most of his indestructible women are either mothers or whores."[35] The critical response to Steinbeck's women in the seventies can be summed up thus: they are found, (a) either in a minority, (b) or having limited role as wives, mothers and whores, (c) or dynamic and memorable meriting keen attention.

The nineteen eighties may partly be recognized as a biographical decade of Steinbeck because as many as four biographies have come out during this period. The more important development in the eighties is the critics' favourable response to Steinbeck's characters including women. Most critics of the decade hail his characters as lifelike and well-developed. For instance, Benson J. Jackson states: "His characters, rather than being imaginative extensions of figures from history and myth, would be patterned after relatives, friends and the people he had observed while he was growing up."[36] Ferrel Keith[37] also emphasizes that his characters come from real-life figures adding that they are well-developed and believable. Refuting Edmund Wilson, John Ditsky contends: "Steinbeck's characters had always possessed a moral dimension, and were never simply helpless pawns in a random choiceless universe." Declining to describe his characters as "types" he maintains that in Steinbeck "facelessness and anonymity are parts of the theme as well as aspects of character."[38] Similar views have also been expressed by Dr. K. Sreenivasan[39] and K.P. Sharma.[40] John H. Timmerman[41] emphasizes that it is only through Steinbeck's characters that we reach the themes of his novels. He finds Steinbeck a born story-teller like Chekhov who has an intuitive sense of character and plot. R.S. Hughes compares Steinbeck with Anderson for his ability to probe the "psychological complexities of seemingly simple characters, who often prove to be extraordinary," and declares that "his characters, including his first memorable women, seem rounder and more believable."[42]

Equally perceptible is the change in the criticism of Steinbeck's women in the present decade. Comparatively, there is a larger number of critics who have written on the subject. Gladstein considers the women in Steinbeck strong to the point of indestructibility, though he feels that the Hemingway's and Steinbeck's fictional world is basically a "masculine" one. R.S. Hughes, on the contrary, shows that Steinbeck's short stories abound with memorable female characters who revolt against the limited roles assigned to them in a patriarchal society. These women may either be called the new women or free-spirited women. Despite the fact, however, that the critics have at long last come to see the importance of women in Steinbeck's fiction and have paid considerable attention to the various aspects of their presence in the fictional world of the novelist, one still feels that full justice has not been done to these characters. As late as 1988, Beth Everest and Judy Weddles[43] speak for many of us when they say that Steinbeck's women on the whole have been neglected by the general school of critics. In their view, the critics have failed to see Steinbeck's women as developed characters who are there not only to add colour to the situation but are part and parcel of the whole system of the novel. Brian St. Pierre is the lone critic who refers to Steinbeck's "dark view of women."[44]

The ordinary criterion of approach to Steinbeck's women that emanates from our resume of the novelist's criticism can be summed up as; (1) Steinbeck's fictional world is basically " masculine" showing a general scarcity of women; (2) the female figures here have been relegated to the background by the more solid attractions of male companionship; (3) limited roles of mothers, wives and whores have been assigned to them; (4) only the novelist's short stories abound with dynamic females.

Thus, one of the limitations of Steinbeck's criticism has been its inability to recognize the various roles the characters play in the fictional world of the novelist. Perhaps it can be granted that women in Steinbeck are not always in the forefront of action in the novel, but there is no denying the fact that they form an important strand in the fabric of the writer's work. Many factors beyond his control might have forced the novelist to reserve a relatively accessory cue to his women. He lived in the time of the Great Depression. The whole Western world was then thrown into great economic, social and political turmoil. Bread-earning had become the chief problem of the day, which at the time was a male province. Economic issues were a male stronghold. Portraying the contemporary American society, a sensitive writer like Steinbeck naturally took up the burning issues of the day, and, consequently, had to give a relatively less important role to his women creations. However, conceding that women do not always dominate the scene in Steinbeck, one cannot in all fairness claim that their role in his world is by any means unimportant. In fact, the critics have failed to recognize the large variety of female characters there is in the short and long fiction of Steinbeck. The variety consists of women belonging to different age groups, different professions and different strata of society. In the Steinbeck canon one comes upon simple but highly moral and sustaining characters like Ma Joad *(The Grapes of Wrath)* as well as noble and conventional figures like Rose of Sharon (The Grapes of Wrath) and Liza Hamilton *(East of Eden)*. There are cunning, clever and unscrupulous women in *Tortilla Flat* as well as complex and amoral characters like Mordeen in the *Burning Bright*. Steinbeck's world throws up unconventional, exceptional characters like Dora Flood *(Cannery Row)*, Fauna and Suzy *(Sweet Thursday)*, alongside the average and commonplace characters like Lizzie and Molly *(East of Eden)*, and Mrs. Meer *(In Dubious Battle)*. We meet here dynamic, radical, rebellious and intellectual women like Una, Dessie, Olive Hamilton *(East of Eden)*, Mrs. Dakin *(In Dubious Battle)*, Annie and Mollie *(The Moon Is Down)*, along with the passive and illiterate characters like the mother of Jim and Liza *(In Dubious Battle)* who have resigned themselves to their fate and cannot think of challenging or resisting the reigning conditions. Here we are exposed to the shockingly unhealthy psyche of women like Cathy Ames in *East of Eden*. The same world also includes the noble and sunny characters like Juana *(The Pearl)*, Marie and Suzanne *(The Short Reign of Pippin IV)*. There are hard-core realists like Camille Oaks *(The Wayward Bus)* contrasted with the day-dreaming visionaries like Clotilde *(The Short Reign of Pippin IV)*. There are tragic characters like Curley's wife in Of *Mice and Men* as well as comic figures like Mrs. Mayor in *The Moon Is Down*, the practical women placed against the idealistic ones. Indeed it is a world full of a rich variety of female figures.

Another failure of Steinbeck criticism has been its insistence that masculinity overshadows femininity in the novelist's world. It may be true in the case of one or two individual works but the contention does not hold good for majority of his novels. A close reading of his works clearly shows that there is no question of women being overshadowed by men here; rather they are complementary to each other. Usually, the novelist views his men or women not as autonomous individuals but as men or women in their mutual relationship with each other. Normally, the women are stronger than their male counterparts. For instance, while in despair, men always turn to women for comfort and support. In fact, Steinbeck's men are generally the dreamers, whereas his women are predominantly realists. In the words of Hayashi Tetsumaro, while the men may be called "theorists," the women are "practical exemplars."[45] Steinbeck's men carry lot of plans and aspirations, but it is only his women who show better capacity for the realization of those dreams and aspirations. In fact, they try to be perfect counterparts to their men by making active contribution to their domestic, social, economic and political life. They are not mere passive observers of but active participants in what goes on around them. Undoubtedly, their prime concern is their duty towards their family, but they are not blind to the happenings around. A living example of it is Ma Joad whose image from that of a simple domestic Women changes into the image of a social saviour by the end of the novel. In Steinbeck women may not be occupying the central position in every work, but by no means can they be dismissed as minor characters.

The critics have also been unfair to the women in Steinbeck in their simplistic descriptions of these characters into clich'ed female types like the mother or the wife. His women move at so many diverse levels of mind and body that their roles cannot be fitted into the clich'ed types. His seemingly simple, dutiful and domestic women participate as actively in the struggle for survival as they do in domestic situations. For instance, we perceive both the angel and the tigress in Ma Joad and Juana. They may not be professional political and social workers, but they never shy away from the hard life in hard times; rather, their involvement in the family affairs in the times of crisis is greater than even those of men. In fact, in some cases the women take up the roles and functions generally attributed to men. For instance, Annie and Mollie are directly involved in the freedom struggle of their country. Similarly, Sister Haycinthe is an informal political advisor to Pippin IV. If no place is given to women as writers or artists, their desire to become so is clearly shown in the ambitious plans of the romantic young Clotilde, daughter of Pippin IV. Curley's wife wanted to be a stage artist. Camille Oaks plays in the 'stags'. Suzanne has been an artist before joining the convent. Steinbeck has depicted numerous aspects of the feminine psychology, including such glimpses as the sex inhibitions of Mrs. Pritchard and Mary Teller, the perverted extremism of Cathy Ames, along with the realism of Mildred Pritchard, Camille Oaks and Sister Haycinthe.

The predominantly accepted notion that only Steinbeck's short stories throng with dynamic feminine characters is a misleading notion, too. There is no denying the fact that his short stories exhibit a variety of new-spirited women, but it is also undisputable that his women of unshakeable strength, unshakeable convictions, the epitomes of female wisdom, exist only in his long novels. Many women such as Alicia and Katherine Sharkwicks in *The Pastures of Heaven*, Elizabeth and Rama in *To a God Unknown*, Ma Joad and Rose of Sharon in

The Grapes of Wrath, Juana in *The Pearl*, Mordeen in the *Burning Bright*, Camille Oaks and Mildred Pritchard in *The Wayward Bus*, Liza Hamilton in *East of Eden* and Suzanne and Clotilde in *The Short Reign of Pippin IV*, etc., are dynamic and memorable characters that demand and merit close study and critical attention. These women may not be called emancipated in the traditional sense of the word, but they are enlightened in their own way. The only difference that remains between the two — that is, women figures in his short and long fiction — is that whereas the former seem to be revolting against the limited roles of wives or mothers assigned to them, the latter seem to find fulfillment in their roles as housewives.

The preconceived nature of the various schools of criticism was responsible for making the Steinbeck critics rather unfair to his women. Since most critics have been guided by their commitment to one or another philosophy of criticism, they have imposed the predetermined categories on these women characters in Steinbeck's work and classified them according to those categories. While the sociological school of critics tends to bypass completely the women in Steinbeck in the process of taking the novelist' reformative aspect into consideration, the archetypal school of critics reduces his women to mere myths and symbols. The biographical critics relate his fiction to his life and identify the characters with their prototypes in real life. The psychological critics probe the minds of his women for various causes of frustration relegating the other aspects to the background. Historian critics analyze the role of his women in relation to the social context of the period and describe them in terms of their counterparts in the social milieu. The marxist school of critics lost interest in the novelist after the 30s, for they thought he had betrayed the socialist cause by not advocating the left cause. Thus, the critical approaches tc Steinbeck's women seem to have hardened into stock descriptions. Each approach is coloured by either personal or extra-literary prejudice. Each has its limitations. Hence the necessity of an approach which should be limited by neither any ideology nor any prejudice and this is what the present research project aims at achieving. In order that the novelist's women characters can be given a fair deal, we need to see them without the eyeglasses of any extra theory or political ideology and to see them as they actually are in the fictional world which is autonomous and should be viewed as such. For more precision, we may say that the project is committing itself to formalist approach, which is by and large an approach free from all extra-literary considerations, pre-conceived notions or complexes on the subject. In brief, the proposed study intends to undertake a dispassionate view of Steinbeck's female world.

The major occupation of Steinbeck regarding his characters, it seems, is to project their function either as individuals or as members of a larger human society, or again, as perfected beings holding an ideal balance between the demands of their individual selves and their obligations towards the larger social setup. Besides, he is trying to relate the human world to its larger surroundings. Not that he subjects his men and women, as does Hardy, to the whims and sports of any cruel gods, but he does not at the same time treat human society or the individuals as something existing in vacuum or in complete isolation. Following this formula of character study in Steinbeck, the present project will try to trace the development of his women as individuals, as members of society and as ideal beings; further, it will seek to analyze the status of Women in relation to man, Women, family and society because it is her response to man,

Women, family and society that is important in Steinbeck's fiction and gives a significant unity to his works. And, finally, this book would take up for discussion at length the relevant themes as in the case of Steinbeck development of theme is closely linked with the development of his characters and his women play an important role in the enhancement of plot and themes like the survival and initiation theme in *The Grapes of Wrath*.

The present book does not claim a comprehensive analysis of the entire richness and complexity of Steinbeck's art. Since its primary concern is the women characters, it would touch upon or include other aspects like technique, style, etc., only so far as they help in highlighting the development of women characters or the status of women in his fiction. The present study as is apparent from the name itself will not include non-fictional works like *Their Blood Is Strong*, *The Log From the Sea of Cortez*, *The Forgotten Village*, *A Russian Journal*, *Viva Zapata*, *The Bombs Away*, *America and Americans*, *Travels with Charley*, *Journal of a Novel.* It would confine itself to only the major novels and short stories, of course, not the unpublished ones, which contain female figures that fit into the devised categories and sub-categories.

Notes

1. Howard Levant, *The Novels of John Steinbeck: A Critical Study* (Columbia: University of Missouri Press, 1974) 1.
2. See, for instance, Edmund Wilson's *"The Californians: Storm and Steinbeck."* The New Republic 103. Dec. 9 (1940); Walter Fuller Taylor's *"The Grapes of Wrath: Reconsidered,"* Mississippi Quarterly XII 1959; Lester Jay Marks', *Thematic Designs in the Novels of John Steinbeck* (1969);

and Roy S. Simmonds', *Steinbeck's Literary Achievement*, Steinbeck Monograph Ser. 6 (Muncie, Indiana: Ball State University, 1976).

3. Barker Fairley, *"John Steinbeck and the Coming Literature,"* Sewanee Review 50 April-June (1942): 148.
4. Woodburn O. Ross, *"John Steinbeck: Naturalism's Priest,"* College English May 1949: 208.
5. ...., *"John Steinbeck: Earth and Stars,"* Studies in Honor of A.H.R. Fairchild (University of Missouri Studies, 1946) 181.
6. Michael F. Moloney, *"Half-Faiths in Modern Fiction,"* The Catholic World Aug. 1950.
7. Edmund Wilson, *"The Californians: Storm and Steinbeck,"* (1940): 784-787.
8. Alfred Kazin, On Native Grounds (1942).
9. E.W. Tedlock, Jr., and C.V. Wicker, introduction Steinbeck and His Critics (Albuquerque: The University of New Mexico Press, 1957) XL-XLI.
10. Charles Poore, introduction The Grapes of Wrath (New York: Harper, 1951) VIII.
11. Peter Lisca, The Wide World of John Steinbeck (New Brunswick, New Jersey: Rutgers University Press, 1958) 207.
12. John S. Kennedy, *"John Steinbeck: Life Affirmed and Dissolved,"* (1951).
13. Frederick J. Hoffman, The Modern Novel in America 1900-1950 (Chicago: Henry Regnery Company, 1951) 149.
14. Richard O'Connor, John Steinbeck (New York: McGraw Hill Book Company, 1970).
15. Lester Jay Marks, Thematic Designs in the Novels of John Steinbeck (1969).
16. Daniel R. Brown *"A Monolith of Logic Against Waves of Nonsense,"* Renascene 16. Fall (1963): 48-51.
17. Peter Lisca, *"Steinbeck and Hemingway,"* Steinbeck Newsletter spring 1969.
18. Warren French, John Steinbeck (New York: Twayne Publishers, Inc., 1961).

19. F.W. Watt, John Steinbeck (Edinburgh: Oliver and Boyd, 1962).
20. Mordecai Marcus, *"The Lost Dream of Sex and Childbirth in 'The Chrysanthemums,' "* Modern Fiction Studies XI Spring (1965).
21. William R. Osborne, *"The Text of Steinbeck's 'The Chrysanthe-mums,"* Modern Fiction Studies 12 Winter (1966).
22. Elizabeth E. McMahan, *" 'The Chrysanthemums': Study of a Women's Sexuality,"* Modern Fiction Studies 14 Winter (1968).
23. Pratt John Clark, John Steinbeck: A Critical Essay (Michigan: Grand Rapids, (1970).
24. Joseph Fontenrose, John Steinbeck: An introduction and Interpretation (1963) 129.
25. Tetsumaro Hayashi, *"Steinbeck's Women in The Grapes of Wrath: A New Perspective,"* KAL 18. 1-4 (1967): 4.
26. Peter Lisca, *"Steinbeck and Hemingway,"* (1969) 35.
27. Paul McCarthy, John Steinbeck (New York: Frederick Ungar Publishing Co., 1980).
28. Richard Peterson, "The Turning Point: The Pastures of Heaven: A Study guide to Steinbeck: A Handbook of His Major Works," ed., Tetsumaro Hayashi (Metuchen, N.J.: The Scarecrow Press, Inc., 1974).
29. Sunita Jain, *John Steinbeck's Concept of man: A Critical Study of His Novels* (New Delhi: New Statesman Publishing Co., 1979).
30. Reloy Garcia, *Steinbeck and D.H. Lawrence: Fictive Voices and the Ethical Imperatives,* Steinbeck Monograph Series 2 (Muncie, Indiana: Ball State University, 1972).
31. Lawrence William Jones, *John Steinbeck as Fabulist* (1973).
32. Roy S. Simmonds, *Steinbeck's Literary Achievement* (1976).
33. Saikichi Nakashima, *"Steinbeck's Women,"* Synopsis of the Reports of the Annual Seminar, KAL 1975.
34. Sandra Beatty, *"A Study of Female Characterization in Steinbeck's Fiction," Steinbeck's Women: Essays in Criticism*, ed., Tetsumaro Hayashi, Steinbeck Monograph Ser. 9 (Muncie, Indiana: Ball State University, 1979).
35. Marilyn L. Mitchell, *"Steinbeck's Strong Women: Feminine Identity in the Short Stories,"* Southwest Review 61 (1976).

36. Mimi Reisel Gladstein, *"Female Characters in Steinbeck: Minor Characters of Major Importance,"* Steinbeck's Women: Essays in Criticism (1979).
37. Jackson J. Benson, *The True Adventures of Steinbeck (*New York : The Viking Press, 1984) 140.
38. Ferrel Keith, *John Steinbeck: The Voice of the Land* (New York: M.Evans and Company, Inc., 1985) 34.
39. John Ditsky, *John Steinbeck: Life, Work and Criticism* (Canada: York Press Ltd., 1985) 26 and 29.
40. Dr. K. Sreenivasan, *"Steinbeck's Image of Man,"* Indian Responses to Steinbeck, ed., R.K. Sharma (Jaipur: Rachna Prakashan, 1986) 66-67.
41. K.P. Sharma, *"John Steinbeck: A Re-appraisal,"* Indian Responses to Steinbeck (1986) 88 and 91.
42. John H. Timmerman, *John Steinbeck's Fiction: The Aesthetics of the Road Taken* (Norman and London: University of Oklahoma Press, (1986) 5.
43. R.S. Hughes, *Beyond 'The Red Pony': A Reader's Guide to Steinbeck's Complete Stories* (Metuchen, N.J.: The Scarecrow Press, Inc., (1987) 3.
44. Beth Everest. and Judy Weddles, *"The Neglected Rib: Women in East of Eden,"* Steinbeck Quarterly XXI. 1-2 Winter-Spring (1988) : 13.
45. Brian St. Pierre, *John Steinbeck: The Californian Years* (San Francisco, California: Chronicle Books, 1983) 35.
46. Tetsumaro Hayashi, *"Steinbeck's Women in The Grapes of Wrath: A New Perspective,"* (1972) 1.

II

Domestic Women : Mothers

Steinbeck's intense love for a harmonious and happy family-life makes him delineate domestic women in his fiction—women fully contented and satisfied with their position in the family. In Steinbeck's fiction, "the family is the basic democratic unit. It is where a true trusteeship is in action. The family ensures the fullest growth of all elements in it. Further, it is where the Women plays a crucial role as mother and wife. Perhaps the strongest sustaining and fostering influence in life that of is Women."[1] Steinbeck's domestic women—mothers, wives, daughters—are primarily tied to their families. Their main occupation is to attend to the physical, mental, moral and spiritual needs of all the members of the family. However, even though the Women's role is restricted to the family only, within the family her positon is in no way inferior to the position of the male. She is the cohesive force in the family. Steinbeck's women are not passive, they are active and assertive. They are not dumb-driven creatures in the home; rather, they dominate in the domestic world. They assume significance in the family because of their deep involvement in the family affairs. Though generally self-effacing, they emerge as a powerful force in crucial situations.

Some of the outstanding traits of Steinbeck's domestic but dynamic women are: enduracne, adaptability, vitality, strength (both moral and physical), indestructibility, durability and indomitability. As John H. Timmerman has remarked, "With the exception of Cathy Ames, Steinbeck observes with appreciation the following character traits in his major female characters: enduracne through adversity, a patient ability to ride with changing circumstances and yet retain an individual point of view, and a loving kindness that, while not immune to adversity, nonetheless finds a straight and sure path through that adversity."[2] Steinbeck has an unswerving faith in Women's ability to absorb tragedy. His women of unshakeable strength unflinchingly undergo pain and hardship providing their men and families with a model of endurance. They show better ability to cope with change and disaster. They are stronger than their male counterparts, who very easily get disheartened in the face of suffering and hardship. In fact, it is when their men are down with grief that they provide leaderhip. They do not show any sign of breakingg down; rather, they shoulder the responsibility of motivating their men-folk. Women's superiority over men in the art of living is well described by Ma Joad in *The Grapes of Wrath* when she says," Man, he lives in Jerks—baby born an' a man dies, an' that's a jerk—gets a farm an' loses his farm, an' that's a jerk. Women, it's all one flow, like a stream, little eddies, little water-falls, but the river, it goes right on." In the words of Hayashi Tetsumaro: "It is the female who drives, cajoles, challenges and scours man in his weakness."[3] Steinbeck's women often possess hidden strength that can emerge in crisis. Never submitting to a situation is the characteristic feature of his women.

Steinbeck's women are intensely and deeply motivatd by

humanitarian impulses. They are strongly religious and their religion enables them to face life with strength and confidence. Theirs is a practical religion that has nothing to do wih rites and rituals. It is a religion of humanity and love, of universal brotherhood. They are not orthodox women of religion. They do not seek guidance from any religious text, nor do they visit any church. They are seldom seen observing any ritual or rite. But they are religiously good and humane. Their goodness and humanitarianism are their articles of faith. They follow them like the commandments of religion. These highly moral and virtuous women exercise a positive influence on their children. Mothers in Steinbeck are a shaping force. They are a channel to bring the erring children back to the right path. They are the prime force of creation. As creators, the makers of home, the care-takers of their children, they bear the responsibility of making them morally and spiritually sound. They initiate them into acts of kindness and goodness. They are the source of physical and spiritual strength to the family. Vigilant mothers in Steinbeck are the custodians of their children's moral and spiritual growth.

Most Steinbeck's women are not formally educated in schools and colleges, but they are well-versed in education of life. They are the epitomes of practical wisdom. They live on a practical plane and have pragmatic and matter-of-fact approach to life. They live life as it comes and do not yearn for what is not. Their education is all imbibed from their surroundings. They are persons of keen insight. As Sandra Beatty has observed, "The most significant quality with which Steinbeck's women are endowed is knowledge—both of their own men and of men generally."[4] They are difinitely superior to men in the art of living.

Steinbeck conceives 'family' as only a unit in one's overall social relationship. Therefore, tied to the family, his women are very much part of the happenings around. The women characters in his world proclaim their seminal importance in group-life. They are dedicatd to the good of the greater number. For them, it is not their own family alone that matters; rather, they view the entire community in a village or settlement as one family. In fact, their feeling of solidarity with other human beings goes beyond these in a village or settlement and encompasses the entire humanity. His domestic women may not hold formal positions in society, they may not be educated in schools and colleges, but they are all capable of social interaction.

Women is a symbol of continuity in Steinbeck, who should engage herself in the propagation of human beings, and function as a perpetuator of the species. In Steinbeck, bearing children is something wonderful, a marvellous experience. In fact, it is considered a somewhat sacred activity. As Joseph Wayne puts it in *To a God Unknown*, "Yes — the child is precious, but not so precious as the bearing of it." Steinbeck's women find fulfillment in childbearing. An expectant mother holds an exalted position in his fiction, and pregnancy is a stage when a mysterious store of knowledge opens up to Women. Unproductivity or sterility leads to abnormality. It is no mere coincidence that sterile women in Steinbeck become highly egocentric; even when sharing the common traits of toughness and strength with all those who are the symbols of positivity, these childless women come to represent the "principle of discontinuity and destruction."[5]

In Steinbeck, women (as well as men) fall into three categories; those who are self-centred, those who are socially-oriented, and those equally interested in personal as well as social affairs. His ideal women are always those who can succcessfully combine personal and social interests and responsibilities. The domestic women in Steinbeck broadly fall into three categories: mothers, wives, and daughters. The three types of women constitute distinct categories having shared traits of character, showing similar responses to familiar domestic situations, and performing common family duties as mothers, wives or daughters.

Mothers

In Steinbeck's fiction the dominant kinship is between mother and children with mother as the centrifugal force in the family. An ideal mother figure who unequivocally comes at the top in his works is Ma Joad, rightly termed as "the soul of American motherhood."[6] She is the central focus of the family from her first appearance until the conclusion of the novel. She stands out as a symbol of positive motherhood. She is enodwed with the qualities of wisdom, patience and love, which are generally attributed to Mother Earth. The very fact that she has not been given any first name and is known as "Ma" only projects her maternal image. Again, her physical appearance emphasizes her maternal role: "Ma" was heavy, but not fat; thick with child-bearing and work. She wore a loose Mother Hubbard of grey cloth in which there had once been coloured flowers ...". Hers is the image of "Lady Bountiful."[7] She is nourisher-feeder, the mother of all, as even Pa Joad calls her "Ma." Being wife and mother, she is the nucleus of the family— a source of the family's physical and spiritual nourishment.

As she comes of Christian family in patriarchal society, where male is the head of the family, Ma Joad pays full respect to the position of Pa Joad. Following the ways of her people, her society, she subordinates herself to Pa Joad, at least at the beginning of the novel. But as ineffectiveness and despondency overpower the whole Joad clan, particularly the men folk, the family authority shifts to Ma Joad. She emerges as the natural leader of the family. As Sam Bluefarb says, "It is Ma Joad who assumes the leadership of, and becomes the moral goad for the family. Where, in an earlier time, the menfolk had led, now the women take over the guidance and running of the family."[8] Even earlier, her position as citadel of the family is recognized by all. Her counsel is sought in the major decisions of the family. In fact, in certain crucial moments it is Ma Joad alone who takes the vital decisions. When the family gathers outside the house to take decision about Casy, Ma goes inside for a minute or so; immediately, the consulations stop and they wait for Ma to come back and take her seat, "for Ma was powerful in the group.". On being asked by Pa Joad whether there would be food enough to feed one extra mouth, she replies, "'It ain't kin we? It's will we?' ". Obviously, it is she who indirectly gives permission for the inclusion of Casy in the family group. Finding the men at their wits' end, she takes over the affairs of the family.

Ma's sole concern after their being uprooted from the farm is to keep the family together. She challenges the patriarchal authority on seeing the family unity at stake. She virtually threatens to hit Pa Joad with a jack handle if Tom is allowed to stay back alone. In most Steinbeck works women assume authority for the good of the greater number. Here Ma Joad challanges patriarchal authority only to prevent the weakening of the group structure, that is the family unit. To quote Joseph Warren Beach , " she is a lower of strength in all that concerns the family welfare, and the great mission of keeping them together and intact."[9] Ma has an irrespressible will to live and acts as a source of strength for the entire family. When menfolk fail to fulfill their role as provider, when they fail to get work in the Government Camp, Ma takes the initiative and makes the family move on. Later, she plans Tom's escape from the peach ranch after he avenges Casy's murder. Handling the family affairs tactfully, she urges Rose of Sharon to feed the starving man in a barn. Thus, Ma's position as citadel of the family is well-earned: "Her hazel eyes seemed to have experienced all possible tragedy and to have mounted pain and suffering like steps into a high calm and a superhuman understanding. She seemed to know, to accept, to welcome her position, the citadel of the family, the strong place that could not be taken."

Ma's trials start with the uprooting of the family. First, she has to part with some of her valuable tokens of the past, but she bears the pain without letting others have the slightest idea of her mental agony. She is well aware of the family's reliance on her as a pillar of strength. It is she on whom the family depends for comfort and solace. It is she from whom the entire family draws courage and inspiration: "And from her great and humble position in the family she had taken dignity and a clean calm beauty. From her position as healer, her hands had grown sure and cool and quiet, from her position as arbiter, she had become as remote and faultless in judgement as a goddess. She seemed to know that if she swayed the family shook, and if she ever really deeply wavered or despaired the family would fall, the family will to function would be gone." Knowing her family's dependence on her, she could not afford to show her pain and anguish: "As feeder, she must be indomitably strong for if the feeder weeknes, the family falls apart."[10] On the occasion of Granma's death, Ma's indomitability, her remarkable courage, and her terrific strength leave everyone wonder struck. Only she could have the courage of lying with the dead body of Granma throughout the night without breaking the news to others, for the family was to cross the deadly desert. In Steinbeck's own words, "The family looked at Ma with a little terror at her strength." Casy, the preacher, asessing the enormity of Ma's deed, is all praise for Ma's touch of love and humanity: "John, there's a Women so great with love—she scares me. Makes me afraid an' mean."

Ma's trials do not stop with the deaths of Granpa and Granma, with the loss of home and tokens of the past. More deaths and departures follow, but Ma remains intact, still providing all with a will to go on: Noah leaves the group; the Wilsons are to be left behind; Connie deserts; the preacher dies; Tom becomes a fugitive; Rose of Sharon's baby is born dead. But all along, in spite of everything, Ma remains strong and steadfast. As Lester Jay Marks rightly observes, "The men of the migrant families, traditionally the leaders, often falter from the great weight of their burden; but women like Ma Joad, trained by years of suffering hardships silently, are prepared to hold the family-group together until the men are once again ready to assume responsibility."[11] Comparing Ma Joad with the heroine of Gorky's *Mother* Tamara Khmelnitskaya says, "Like the heroine of Gorky's *Mother* Ma Joad revealed the same daily heroism in the face of a terrible life, the same growing understanding of reality, magnificent talent for enduring sorrow, and readiness to suffer.[12]

Throughout the novel Ma Joad functions as a nurturing

mother to all, and she nurtures not only her own children but anyone in need of care. She mothers Granpa and Granma, too. She is unfailing in discharging her domestic duties. Tenderly and affectionately she attends to the needs of all the members of the family, from Granpa to Ruthie. Like a mother she looks after Granpa, so much so that she even buttons his pants as if he were a little boy. After Granpa's death, Ma's sole concern is to keep Granma intact. She looks after Granma during her illness as a mother would her own children. Although she herself is dead tired she patiently serves Granma. She relieves uncle John of his mental agony. As Earth-Mother, as a goddess, she ladles out stew for the starving children who gather around her kettle, even though she does not have enough food to feed her own family. She is always ready to share whatever little she has. As Jones puts it, she is "an earth-mother whose less intellectualized actions reveal the same kind of sharing and suffering as Casy's."[13]

As mother to her own children, Ma Joad takes up the role of a tutor who initiates Tom Joad and Rose of Sharon into love and goodness making them perform little acts of kindness. She goes into every minute detail of the life of her children. She has to find food and clothing for and give direction to Ruthie and Winfield, who despite her efforts seem to grow into wild creatures. Ma must persuade A1 not to elope with the girl he loves and wants to marry, for she wants A1 to bring her and her family into a larger communal orbit with the Joads. On Tom's return from the Jail, her first worry is whether her son cherishes any ill-will or hatred for anyone. After being uprooted, her sole concern has been to keep the family together. But when finally the time comes for Tom to part with the family for the welfare of the larger community, Ma Joad, "the essence of wisdom and right judgement,"[14] bids farewell to her son without creating much fuss over it. Transcending her narrow personal interests to save her family, she prepares herself for any sacrifice for the good of the larger community. Earlier, she cares for the "family"; now, she cares for the needy.

As mother to her young daughter, Rose of Sharon, she functions on so many levels, all affirmative. Self-centred, whining, grumbling, Rose of Sharon's initiation starts when Ma persuades her to fan the old, dying Granma. Her training in hardships starts with her desertion by Connie. With the comforting care of Ma Joad, the once grumbling Rose of Sharon is slowly converted into a helping companion. In spite of her ill-health, she helps Ma with cooking and washing of dishes. She insists on picking up cotton to add up to the family income. Ma gradually transfers her responsibility of serving the suffering humanity to Rose of Sharon. Ma passes the torch to the young lady in two symbolic scenes: first, Ma's offering of her earrings to Rose would automatically mean the piercing of her ears, which involves the act of bearing pain and suffering. Rose would have to prove herself that she is prepared to assume Ma's responsibility. Secondly, with her final act of feeding a starving old man, she makes her place with Ma. She becomes an extension of Ma, the earth-goddess, the nourisher-feeder, the one who sees to the feeding of family and strangers. Through the mother-daughter relationship Steinbeck seems to suggest "a pattern of continuity and resurrection" and by the end of the novel, the daughter "is ready to take her place beside Ma as a pillar of the family."[15] Just as Jim Casy's spirit is perpetuated by Tom Joad, so Ma's enters her daughter, Rose of Sharon, at the conclusion of the novel.

Ma's journey of transcendentalism starts at a very early stage with the inclusion of Casy among the family members.

Innumerable sufferings—both physical and mental—work as purifier. Overwhelming odds purify Ma Joad's soul, mind and body. By the end of the novel, her image from that of a natural leader turns into that of a saviour of suffering humanity.

Steinbeck's mother figures are usually endowed with a number of sustaining qualities which provide them with endurance and make them indispensable and also superior to men in the art of living. Ma Joad reaffirms this idea when she says that women show better abilities to cope with change and disaster: "Women got all her life in her arms. Man got it all in his head." Another mother figure, radiating strength to others like Ma Joad and representing Ma Joad's qualities of endurance and indestructibility, is Rama in *To a God Unknown*. She, too, is an earth-mother figure, a representative of the eternal maternal, acting as the matriarch on the farm. She exercises a goddess-like authority over all coming within her territory. All the children on the farm intuitively recognize a mother in her. As her authority extends beyond her role as a "good and efficient midwife," "She automatically took charge of all children who came near her." She is not only a nurturing soul to them all but also a custodian of their moral and spiritual growth. Unlike Ma Joad, Rama, like a disciplinarian, does the job with an iron hand. She is "an utter terror to evil-doing children ... The children adored Rama when they had been good, for she knew how to stroke the tender places in the soul. Her praise would be as delicate and sharp as her punishment was terrible." Rama metes out reward and punishment alike. Like all other Steinbeck's domestic women, she is a Women of steady values; laws never change for her; she represents an everlasting standard, "for the laws of Rams never changed, bad was bad and bad was punished, and good was eternally, delightfully good." Justice-loving Rama does not use different scales for measuring good or bad in her own daughters or in the children of her brothers-in-law. She judges her daughters by equally harsh standards "although she never whipped her three little daughters, they went in fear of her displeasure, for she could find a soft spot in the soul and punish there." Her earth-mother image is emphasized in the novel when she becomes, after the death of Elizabeth, a natural mother, a care-taker of Joseph's and Elizabeth's son: "Rama's symbolic role comes when she takes the son of Joseph and Elizabeth to raise as her own."[16] She is the preserver of the species as she reproduces herself. As Gladstein puts it, "her priorities are set by her role as preserver of the species. Demeter-like she reproduces herself; Rama has three daughters."[17]

Acting as mother even to her husband, Rama is a Women of sharp insight who has a thorough knowledge of her own husband as well as men in general. Like a dutiful wife and an affectionate mother she attends to the needs of her husband without expecting anything in return: "she understood Thomas, treated him as though he were an animal, kept him clean and fed and warm and didn't often frighten him." She keeps her husband tenderly and preserved him as a mother would do a small child. Rama's life-preserving role is seen in relation to other members of the family. She preserves life like "an incarnation of the Hindu God Vishnu,"[18] and acts as a midwife to the child of Joseph and Elizabeth. After Elizabeth's death, she comes to the rescue of Joseph Wayne and relieves him of the mental agony caused by death: "Rama is like the glade, with Elizabeth dead, there is still Rama, the great earth-mother who lives on, fulfilled by men and fulfilling man."[19] She comes to Joseph as a healer and a surrogate mate. Acting her incarnation of the Great Mother role she draws his pain into herself: "The long deep river of sorrow is diverted into me..."

Rama is a strong Women, unfaltering and unwavering. Her superiority is recognized not only by the children and male members of the family, but even by the female members who feel safe in her presence: "Elizabeth felt the strength of Rama and knew she should resent it, but it was a safe, pleasant thing to have this sure Women by her side." Rama is as protective, as comforting, as consoling to Elizabeth as she would be to her own daughters or to her husband, or to the other children. in thc family. Elizabeth is confused on her first arrival on the farm. She is almost on the verge of tears when Rama comes to her rescue and makes her feel comfortable. Rama is not only a mother to Elizabeth but also a good teacher, making her learn things naturally without the slightest show of her superiority over Elizabeth and also without giving her the impression of being critical: "Rama was a teacher, a tactful Women, for she could show Elizabeth methods of doing things about the house without seeming to criticise Elizabeth's methods."

Like Ma Joad, she is an epitome of practical wisdom. When life in the valley is completely unbearable, when life has departed from the valley and Joseph insists on staying in the valley, Rama remains unmoved. She decides to leave the valley without Joseph along with her children and her husband and the remaining animals. Hope for the future persists in Rama; she is the sole person on whom the future existence of the Wayne family depends: "If there is any hope for the future of the Wayne family, it is embodied in Rama, who takes her own children and Joseph's child to care for and raise."[20] Throughout the novel, she remains a life-sustaining force, imparting strength to others, radiating her sublimity into others.

Anothe mother figure in Steinbeck's fiction, besides Ma Joad and Rama, is Katherine Sharkwicks in *The Pastures of Heaven*. She is a symbol of female imperishability and invincibility. Taken at face value, she is very submissive in the begining. She is like an inanimate object, a stone, whose value cannot be understood until the time of crisis: "Her husband never treated her as a human, nevr spoke of his hopes or thoughts or failures of his paper wealth nor of the peach crop." But this seemingly simple Women can be a fiery ball, like Ma Joad, if the situation so demands. For example, on being pestered by her husband on the point of their daughter's chastity, she gets irritated and snubs him:

> One day when Alice was sixteen, Shark went to his wife with a worried look on his face. 'You know we really can't tell if she's all right—that is —we couldn't really be sure unless we took her to a doctor.'
>
> For a moment Katherine stared at him, trying to realize what the words meant. Then she lost her temper for the first time in her life. 'You're a dirty, suspicious skunk, she told him. 'You get out of here. And if you ever talk about it again, I'll—I'll go away.' Shark was a little astonished, but not frightened, at her outburst. He did, however, give up the idea of a medical examination, and merely contented himself with his monthly questions.

The full potential of her hidden strengths, her maternal instincts, is realized only when she comes to her husband as a comforting soul. Caressing motherly instinct has always been dominant in Katherine Sharkwicks, but it comes to limelight only when her husband comes to need it. The once submissive Women becomes all powerful, soothing and comforting when her husband loses his vitality after being publicly exposed. She becomes her husband's Great Mother and "with a sure hand, took Shark's head in her lap. This was instinct, and the same sure, strong instinct set her hand to stroking Shark's forehead. His body seemed boneless with defeat." In her husband's hour of defeat, she becomes a symbol of hope and strength. When he gets weak, she becomes strong: "Shark's renewed vigour results from the strength conferred on him by his once docile wife, Katherine, who grows in strength as her husband weakens .... Katherine breaks through to a recognition of her husband's needs... and she dispels her husband's misery and forces him to face life squarely for the first time."[21] Katherine's strength is not to gain power over her husband; it is to infuse him with a renewed vigour, a renewed energy, and a strong will to go on: "Katherine stroked his head gently and the great genius contined to grow in her. She felt larger than the world. The whole world lay in her lap and she comforted it. Pity seemed to make her huge in stature. her soothing breasts yearned towards the woe of the world." Katherine intuitively knows her power over her husband at the moment. But the eternal mother, the nourisher-feeder, instead of becoming strong herself, feeds her strength into her husband just as a mother's nourishment is drained into the child: "Suddenly the genius in Katherine becomes power and the power gushed in her body and flooded her. In a moment she knew what she was and what she could do." Like all other Steinbeck's mother figures, Katherine's function is to become a stream of strength from where men draw their energy and regain power to fit into their role of worker-provider. As Katherine's energy funnels into her husband, he becomes his usual self, forgetful of Katherine. But there is no doubt that she is sure to show herself again when her man needs her.

Katherine's indomitability, her earth-mother image, her hidden strength, are all suggested in the very beginning through her connection with nature: "Katherine was not pretty, but she had the firm freshness of a new weed and the bridling vigour of a young mare." She displays her practical wisdom in the way she protects her young but slow-minded daughter and takes to serving her in the minutest detail: "As for Katherine, the constantly increasing beauty of Alice augmented her misgiving. Destiny was storing strength for a more violent blow. She became the slave of her daughter, hovered about and did little services such as one might accord an invalid who is soon to die." She is a caring mother. On the insistence of Alice, she takes her to the ball against the wishes of her husband. For the sake of her daughter's happiness she risks the wrath of her husband.

Juana in The Pearl also belongs to the same class of mother-figures to which Ma Joad, Rama and Katherine belong. She represents Steinbeck's theme of endurance and strength in women. From the beginning, she makes her appearance in the role of a life-preserver for her beloved ones: "From beginning to end, devoted to the preservation of her beloved ones, man and child."[22] She is a rare combination of a devoted wife and a caring mother. Her image of a watchful Great Mother is emphasized in the very beginning: "Juana's eyes were open too. Kino could never remember seeing them closed when he awakened. Her dark eyes made little reflected stars. She was looking at him as she was always looking at him when he awakened." She is always on her guards. She is a caring, loving mother whose sole concern is to keep her family intact, to protect her man and child from every possible evil. She "symbolizes the positive and nurturing qualities of Women, the omnipresent mother, always on guard to protect her own."[23] The very first thing she does in the morning is to go to her child to reassure him of her comforting presence: "On her hard bare feet she went to the hanging box where Coyotito slept, and she leaned over and said a little reassuring word. Coyotito looked up for a moment and closed his eyes and slept again.". Juana's fostering role comes into prominence when she sees a scorpion heading towards the child's box. She immediately gets alarmed about some secret danger to the family. Her spontaneous reaction is to cast a magic spell on the child to guard him against evil: "Under her breath Juana repeated an ancient magic to guard against such evil, and on top of that she uttered a Hail Mary between clenched teeth." As the family is exposed to crisis after crisis, Juana's resourcefulness and instinctive wisdom become more and more apparent. Juana's practical wisdom, her watchfulness, her presence of mind, are definitely unique. When the baby is bitten it is only Juana who sucks out the poison: "Juana had the bady in her arms now. She found the puncture with redness starting from it already. She put her lips down over the puncture and sucked hard and spat and sucked again while Coyotito screamed. Kino hovered; he was helpless, he was in the way." The invicible and imperishable spirit of Juana fills everyone with wonder. She insists on calling a doctor for her sick child, an unusual thing for their community. Even Kino admires the iron strength of his patient and fragile wife.

Ability to survive is one of the significant characteristics of Steinbeck's women. they have the courage to remain balanced and unshattered in the face of hardships. When the doctor refuses to come, it is the resourceful mother, Juana, who persuades her husband to procure a pearl for the doctor's treatment of her sick child. She does not lose her patience and presence of mind. She is not a docile Women who would waste her time on weeping;

rather, she is a Women of action. She calmly applies her home-made formulas on the wound. First, it is the sucking of posion, and then the poultice made of brown seaweeds. Gradually, the swelling subsides, the redness goes, and the baby is saved. Juana saves the baby but destiny works against both the baby and the family. The song of evil, the evil of the pearl, follows and the child is killed ultimately by the chasers. Juana's untiring patience is as matchless as Ma Joad's. She keeps her calm and becomes a protective mother-goddess to her man who needs comfort. Now it is the man who is to be protected against evil, for if the man lives on more children will follow.

Juana becomes a source of strength for her man who is running away from the pearl-buyers. He is confused and frightened but Juana transmutes her strength into Kino: "He looked then for weakness in her face, for fear or irresolution, and there was none. Her eyes were very bright. He shrugged his shoulders helplessly then, but he had taken strength from her." When he wavers in his determination, she encourages him: "When his determination flags, she encourages him, when the situation becomes dangerous, she will not leave him, though he tries to make her go."[24] But Juana's unbelievable display of mental strength and practical wisdom is seen at the end of the novel when the worse has happened. The child is killed by the trackers. It is here that she acts like Ma Joad and Hemingway's Pilar and lets his man regain his sense of dignity, who is to be filled with renewed strength. Realizing the futility of his ambition and the danger of Juana's dreads coming true, Kino offers her the pearl to throw back into the sea. However, rather than throw back the pearl into the Sea, she makes her man accept his position as head of the family and gives it back to him to do the job himself. Thus, she helps him maintain his dignity as man. Dr. K. Sreenivasan says of Juana: "The growth and maturation of Kino's personality would never have taken place but for the preservative role played by Juana."[25] Juana, as a representative of Womenkind, plays the role of fostering and preserving the strength and dignity of man.

Like Juana, Liza Hamilton in *East of Eden* has incredible strength of character. She commands respect from her own people as well as from others: "Liza enjoyed universal respect because she was a good Women and raised good children. She could hold up her head anywhere. Her husband and her children and her grand-children respected her. There was a nail-hard strength in her, a lack of any compromise, a rightness in the face of all-opposing wrongness,which made you hold her in a kind of awe but not in warmth." Like Rama Wayne, she is a Women of set ideas and values. Her sense of morality remains unchanged with the temporal changes. Good is eternally good and bad is eternally bad for her: "Liza had a finely developed sense of sin. Idleness was a sin, and card playing, which was a kind of idleness to her. She was suspicious of fun, whether it involved dancing or singing or even laughter." Her inadaptability to change, makes others stand in awe of her. Her physical features are as stern as her ideas: "Her head was small and round and it held small, round convictions." Liza is a strong Women in the puritan tradition.

Liza's image of a mother-figure is emphasized in the novel time and again. She is introduced in the novel as a dutiful and efficient mother, looking after her household duties unfailingly: "Liza was a good plain cook, and her house—it was always her house—was brushed and pummelled and washed." Her effectual, unfaltering methods of looking after the minute details of the house and the people living in it evoked awe and admiration among those around her: ... it was almost a miracle how liza, skinny little biddy that she was, produced them year after year and fed them, baked bread, made their clothes, and clothed them with good manners and iron morals too." A mother of iron morals herself, she stamps the same iron morals on her children. Her mother-image is furthr emphasized by Samuel Hamilton who calls her 'mother' all the time. It is really admirable how a Women having no knowledge of books except the Bible could influence her children so deeply. All her knowledge is imbided from her reading of the Bible: "In that one book she had her history and her poetry, her knowledge of people and things, her ethics, her morals, and her salvation."

Liza's strength of character and practical wisdom come out remarkably on the occasion of Una's death, which leaves Samuel completely shattered. But Liza keeps her calm. Her strong faith in the just ways of God is her source of strength: "Liza who surely loved her family as deeply as did her husband, was not destroyed or warped. Her life continued evenly. She felt sorrow but she survived it." She is more practical than her husband, a realist placed against a dreamer: "Samuel's wife, a small, unsmiling flint like who all her life has gotten along with her accentric husband better than might have been expected, judging by her austere morals.[26] Liza is there to support and console her disheartened husband in his hour of agony. Liza's strong faith makes her accept the world easily: "I think perhaps Liza accepted the world as she accepted the Bible, with all of its paradoxes and reverses. She did not like death but she knew it existed, and when it came it did not surprise her." Like Ma Joad and Juana, she has endless patience to endure suffering. Her mountain-like courage is well expressed in the conversation between. Will and Adam on the occasion of Samuel's death:

Will leaned back in his chair and an affectionate smile came on his face. 'She's a remarkable Women,' he said. 'She's like a rock. I think back on all the hard times we had, and we had plenty of them. My father wasn't very practical. He was always of in the clouds or buried in a book. I think my mother held us together and kept the Hamiltons out of the poor house.'

'She's a fine Women,' said Adam.

'Not only fine. She's strong. She stands on her two feet. She's a tower of strength. Did you come back to Olive's house after the funeral?'

'No, I didn't.'

'Well, over a hundred people did. And my mother fried all that chicken and saw that everybody had enough.'

'She didn't.'

'Yes, she did. And when you think it was her own husband.'

'A remarkale Women,' Adam repeated Will's phrase.

'She's practical. She knew they had to be fed and she fed them.'

'I guess she'll be all right, but it must be a great loss to her.'

'She'll be all right,' Will said. 'And She'll outlive us all, little tiny thing that she is.'

Whole of Liza has been packed here in these few lines. A most significant trait Liza possesses like all Steinbeck's women is the thorough knowledge of her own husband and persons in general. She has that keen insight of seeing beyond the surface. Intuitively she sees through Cathy and realizes that she is a completely bad Women.

Mama Torres in the short story called "*Flight*" is yet another example of unparalleled maternal figures. A model of unending endurance, she shares the strength of Liza Hamilton. She is a Women who believes in the just ways of God. She is a fatalist like Liza Hamilton and accepts willingly whatever life grants her. Her hardships start at avery early stage with the death of her husband: "Mama Torres, a lean dry Women with ancient eyes, had ruled the farm for ten years, ever since her husband tripped over a stone in the field." For ten years she keeps the family going. She successfully accomplishes her dual role of a nourisher-feeder and worker—provider-providing bread and clothes to her sons and daughter. Simultaneously, she bears the responsibility of their moral and spiritual growth. But her trials do not stop here. The hardest test of her ability to endure comes when her eldest son Pepe reaches manhood. Mama Torres has dreaded the day always, and she has intuitively known that the day of Pepe's maturity would be the doom's day. Her worst fears come true when in a party in the town Pepe kills a man on being challenged. Mama Torres comes to know that the time of final parting with the second man of the house has come. She calmly accepts it: "Yes, thou art a man, my poor little Pepe. Thou art a man. I have seen it coming on thee. I have watched you throwing the knife into the post, and I have been afraid." His departure to an unknown fortune is extremely painful for her, but she would not demonstrate her agony.

To escape imprisonment, Pepe is bound to run away. Mama summons all her courage and the necessary strength to permit her first born to move to the unknown, perhaps his death. A nurturing soul, Mama provides for his basic needs, giving him food, water, blankets and a gun. She does not allow herself to break down in the presence of Pepe lest he should become weak.

Keeping a bold face, like Ma Joad, she endures the unendurable, displaying exemplary strength. Pepe looks into her face for sympathy: "Pepe turned back to Mama. He seemed to look for a little softness, a little weakness in her. His eyes were searching, but Mama's face remained fierce. She exhilarates strength into whosever turns to her for support. As Gladstein says, "Mama Torres is controlled enough not to break in Pepe's presence. She plays the role much like Ma Joad and others of Steinbeck's indestructible women, of inspiring strength in those who look to her."[27] It is only after Pepe's departure that Mama Torres breaks down and makes a public display of her mental agony. She mourns the inevitable death of Pepe for some time, which is more or less a ritual, and then goes into the house shutting the door after her: "When the grey shape of Pepe melted into the hillside and disappeared, Mama relaxed. She began the high whining keen of the death wail. 'Our beautiful—our brave,' she cried. 'Our protector, our son is gone.' Emilio and Rosy moaned beside her. 'Our beautiful—our brave, he is gone.' It was the formal wail. It rose to a high piercing whine and subsided to a moan. Mama raised in three times and then she turned and went into the house and shut the door." Her gesture is a clear indication of Mama's invincibility. She would be the same Mama Torres, nourishing and sustaining the next generation, looking after the needs of her remaining two children and transferring her inaccessible spirit to her daughter, Rosy.

Mother in "*The Red Pony*" shares the sharp insight, wisdom and strength of all Steinbeck's careful mothers. Like Ma Joad, she has not been given any first name just to reinforce her mother-image. She keeps a guarded look on her only son's mental and physical growth. She is worried about everything concerning her son—from his physical appearance to his education. Ordinarily, she is a hard task master and would like to keep her son disciplined. She would not stand any laxity on the part of his son in discharging his duties. But when she finds her son in agony, she is as tender as any of Steinbeck's mother could be. She becomes a caring mother to relieve the agony of Jody when the latter's pony is unwell: "She held his chin in her hard hand and brushed the tangled hair out of his eyes and she said: 'Don't worry about the pony. He'll be all right. Billy's as good as any horse-doctor in the country." Internally she is happy on seeing Jody getting worried about his pony. She is contented that Jody is growing into a sensitive boy who can feel the suffering of others: "His mother looked after him for a moment and then went quietly back to her work. Her eyes were brooding and kind. Now and then her mouth smiled a little but without changing her eyes at all." She is a Women of keen insight and deep understanding. She knows the mental state of her son concerning the sick pony, so she would not bother him with questions: "His mother fed him and put dry clothes on. She didn't question him. She seemed to know he couldn't answer questions.

Usually, she is caring mother to her husband, too, never complaining, never grudging. But she is not passive. Like Katherine Sharkwicks, she can go to the extent of even snubbing her husband if the situation so demands. And when such a situation does arise, "Carl turned his eyes away from her anger. He could be stern with her most of the time, but when occasionally her temper arose, he could not combat it." She is stern when sternness is necessary, but soft when softness is required. She has the practical wisdom of Ma Joad. She immediately changes her tone from a stern Women to a tactful wise Women, becasue she knows that to welcome her father in the house, her husband shall have to be handled tactfully: "She had caught Carl, caught him and entangled him in her soft tone." Like all other Steinbeck's mothers, she has transmuted her compassionate and hospitable spirit into her only son, Jody who attends and listens to his grandpa's talk tenderly. She is a nurturing mother figure whose sole concern is to give comfort to everyone around.

Among the mother figures of Steinbeck, Mother Morgan in *Cup of Gold* is as practical and strongminded a Women as any other. Perhaps she is the only practical person placed against a pack of dreamers. Throughout the day she keeps herself busy in discharging her household duties: "Mother Morgan was too busy with the day itself to be bothered with the foolishness of abstractions. Someone in the family had to be practical or the thatch would blow away—and what could you expect of a pack of dreamers like Robert and Gwenliana and her son Henri?" Mother Morgan is the most dreaded and the most loved person in the home and neighbourhood: "And all of the family loved Mother Morgan and feared her and got in her way." Even Dafydd, an old friend of Robert, fears Mother Morgan: "Mother Morgan freightened him as she had when he was a tow headed farm boy." She is a dominating as well as a caring mother at the same time. At first, she resists Henri's going away but at last resigns herself to his decision and does not make a show of her feelings. But after his departure, she becomes almost a dumb creature. She is thoroughly shattered by the shock of separation: "She did not weep nor move nor even seem to breathe." Morgan's mother-image is emphasized by the fact that she is known as "mother" by all.

Still another figure in the family of Steinbeck's mothers is the unnamed Lee's mother in *East of Eden*, who is an angel of love an loyalty. She is a strong Women who draws her strength from her instinct of love. Her instinctive power of love makes her imperishable. As Lee recalls her, "She was a strong Women, and I believe a strong Women may be stronger than a man, particularly if she happens to have love in her heart. I guess a loving Women is almost indestructible." Her devotion and loyalty to her husband and child is matchless. In order to remain near her husband, she always appears in men's clothes. She does not disclose her illness and pregnancy to her husband until they have completed the journey. She is so considerate that she does not want to burden her husband with more worries. She endures the sufering—mental as well as physical—alone: "And she didn't want to burden my father with more worries." For the sake of her husband and her unborn child she works as a labourer and, for the purpose, she keeps her identity a secret. In spite of her advanced stage of pregnancy and ill-health, she does as much manual work as a man would do. Admiring the muscular strength of his mother Lee says: "A Women's muscles harden just as a man's do and my mother had a muscular spirit too. She did the pick and shovel work expected of her, and it must have been dreadful." She is a courageous Women. There is the fear of her identity being disclosed any moment, but she is not frightened at all. She boldly figures out a plan with her husband for the birthing. She collects every scrap of cloth to make garments for the unborn child: "And my mother collected every tattered scrap of cloth she could find and unravelled edges to make thread and sewed this ragbag together with a splinter to make swaddling clothes for me." Their plans for the birthing are dashed to the ground when Lee's mother becomes a victim of men's lust. Her remarkable courage and her devotion to the child are so great that even in her dying hours she gives instructions to her husband for saving the child: "She had not even eyes to see out of, but her mouth still moved and she gave him his instructions. My father clawed me out of the tattered meat of my mother with his fingernails. She died on the shale in the afternoon." Lee's mother's whole character is aptly summed up by Beth Everest and Judy Weddles in the following words: "Of the women presented Lee's mother is perhpaps the strongest, both physically and in her devotion to her husband and child. The portrait of her is one of unswerving love, raised to a level of nobility and martyrdom. She symbolized the unsurmountable strength women can, and in *East in Eden*, do have."[28] These indestructible maternal figures of Steinbeck show diversity and yet at the same time similarity in their characters.

If the novelist's ideal mother figures symbolize the principle of continuity, his "inferior" or "imperfect" mother figures represent the principle of discontinuity or destruction; if the former are the model of patience and sacrifice, the latter are self-centred ego-centrics. The negative mother figures are shallow, self-indulgent and extrovert. Although extremily upsets the whole balance leading to some abnormal trait in their characters, the imperfect maternal figures of Steinbeck do share some traits with the ideal mother figures, such as , enduracne, indestructability and courage. However, in the ultimate analysis, these qualities lead them and those around them nowhere, indeed. For instance, in *The Pastures of Heaven* Mrs. Munroe's extrovert nature and even her extreme concern for the downtrodden of the society prove a disaster both for the family as well as for society. She is kind, helping and generous, but she lacks the practical wisdom of Steinbeck's indomitable mothers. In her efforts to help others she always gets to destroy them. She takes pity on Robbie Maltby and offers him good clothes to wear. But the way the whole thing is done makes the Maltbys' conscious of their poverty for the first time and they leave the valley in shame. Thus, Mrs. Munroe becomes responsible for their banishment from the valley. Even as mother she fails to exercise any positive influence on her children. Her lack of practical wisdom results in the hysterical fits of Manny, the youngest son in the family, making the child invalid for ever: "Manny became terrified of the operation, and his mother, seeing this, had used it as a deterrent threat when he was bad. Now, a mention of having his adenoids removed made Manny hysterical with terror." Mrs. Munroe with her tactless and unwise behaviour hampers the natural growth of her own son by making him scared of his operation. The society as well as the family suffer because of her uncanny behaviour. She is an utter failure on both the fronts. In sharp contrast to Ma Joad, she radiates suffering.

Similarly, even though Helen Van Deventer shares the indomitability of Steinbeck's great mothers—like she shares with Juana her power of enduracne—there is a great difference between the sufferings of the two. For instance, whereas Juana is a victim of circumstances, Helen's suffering is all self-imposed. Helen is self-indulgent and suffers from a masochistic strain in her character—that is, she enjoys suffering. As says Richard Peterson: "She discovers a self-satisfying pleasure in pain and misery, and she thrives upon the tragic."[29] She is a Women of sick mentality who recreates her unreal suffering over a dead husband for almost fourteen years, presenting herself all the time as a living image of mourning. "Like her daughter Hilda, she is insane; she clings to the past and perpetuates it. After the death of her husband, she could very easily put her insane daughter into mental hospital. But she does not do it because

Hilda's insanity serves as a constant ordeal for Helen"[30] who has the "morbid need to endure tragedy."[31] She lives in her world of make-believe and self-deception.

Still another negative mother figure in Steinbeck's fiction is Mrs. Pritchard in *The Wayward Bus*, whose self-centredness makes her daughter an alien to her. Young Mildred, a realist, hates her mother for her hypocrisy and her sex inhibitions. The latter fails to keep a check over her young daughter's sexual ambitions who gets involved with Juan Chicoy in a pre-marital sexual relationship. The same way, Mrs. Ames in *East of Eden* lacks the keen perception and practical wisdom of the positive mother figures like Ma Joad, Juana and Liza Hamilton. As a result, her daughter Cathy Ames turns a monster. Abra's mother, Mrs. Bacon,also fails to give that love and affection to her young daughter which Liza Hamilton and Ma Joad shower on their children. Abra gets a spiritual mother, the custodian of her moral values, in the Chinese cook, Lee. Lee becoms her symbolic mother. Mrs Marie Pippin in *The Short Reign of Pippin IV* and Mrs. Mary Hawley in *The Winter of Our Discontent* fail to exercise any constructive influence on their children. These mother figures may share one or the other positive trait of Steinbeck's ideal mothers, but definitely they are far from being satisfactory figures.

Thus, women as mothers in Steinbeck's fiction emerge as strong-willed characters having great capacity for endurance and deep reserves of compassion. The best in them comes out in times of crisis. Largely belonging to the unpriviledged lower sections of society, they are given to endure long spans of suffering without any questioning or complaint. One can compare them with the common characters in William Wordsworth who are also given to accept suffering with exceptional courage. However, whereas in Wordsworth, these characters are suffering individuals, in Steinbeck, they are an integral part of suffering masses, who are struggling against the natural as well as the man-made odds of life. Mostly belonging to the peasant stock, these women are not only physically sturdy, they are equally tough in mind and spirit. What is conspicuous about these women is their ability to rise to the occasion and provide leadership to the suffering male-members of their respective families. In fact, Steinbeck enlarges these mother figures from ordinary mothers into symbolic and mythical mothers of mankind. They come to represent the source of sustenance for the suffering humanity and a symbol of hope for the future of mankind. What is positive about Steinbeck's mother figures is that they always emerge stronger from the struggle. The longer the struggle and the suffering, the more hardened and composed these women become. Though they are facing the evils of affluent society, the ills of agrarian culture, untouched, unaffected they go on fighting against them. Unfailingly they face the trials of life.

Notes

1. Dr. K. Sreenivasan, *John Steinbeck: A Study of His Novels* (Trivendrum: College Book House, 1980) 190.
2. John H. Timmerman, *John Steinbeck's Fiction: The Eesthetics of the Road Taken* (1986) 112-113.
3. Tetsumaro Hayashi, "Steinbeck's" Women in *The Grapes of Wrath* (1967) 3.
4. Sandra Beatty, *"A Study of Female Characterization in Steinbeck's Fiction"* (1979) 3.
5. Tetsumaro Hayashi, *"Steinbeck's Women in The Grapes of Wrath"* (1967) 49.

6. Maxwell Geismer, *"John Steinbeck: Of Wrath or Joy,"* Writers in Crisis: The American Novel 1925-1940 (1942) rpt. in Agnes Mcneill Donohue, ed., A Casebook on The Grapes of Wrath (New York: Crowell, 1968) 137.
7. Mimi Reisel Gladstein, *The Indestructible Women in Faulkner,* Hemingway and Steinbeck (1986) 78.
8. Sam. Bluefarb, *"The Joads: Flight into the Social Soul,"* The Escape Motif in the American Novel (Ohio State University Press) 105.
9. Joseph Warren Beach, *"John Steinbeck: Art and Propaganda,"* Steinbeck and His Critics (1957) 253.
10. John H. Timmerman, *John Steinbeck's Fiction: The Aesthetics of the Road Taken* (1986) 122.
11. Lester Jay Marks, *Thematic Designs in the Novels of John Steinbeck* (1969) 76.
12. James W. Tuttleton, *"Steinbeck in Russia: The Rhetoric of Praise and Blame,"* A Casebook On The Grapes of Wrath (1968) 247.
13. Lawrence William Jones, *Steinbeck as Fabulist* (1973) 17.
14. Maurice Sands, An Outline of the Modern American Novel (1946) 117.
15. Mimi Reisel Gladstein, *Steinbeck's Indestructible Women in Faulkner,* Hemingway and Steinbeck (1986) 81.
16. Lester Jay Marks, *Thematic Designs in the Novels of John Steinbeck* (1969) 44.
17. Mimi Reisel Gladstein, *The Indestructible Women in Faulkner,* Hemingway and Steinbeck (1986) 97.
18. Peter Lisca, *John Steinbeck: Nature and Myth* (New York: Thomas Y. Crowell Company, 1978) 39.
19. Lester Jay Marks, *Thematic Designs in the Novels of John Steinbeck* (1969) 44.
20. Mimi Reisel Gladstein, *The Indestructible Women in Faulkner,* Hemingway and Steinbeck (1986) 97.
21. Richard Astro, *John Steinbeck and Edward F. Ricketts: The Shaping of a Novelist* (Minneapolis: The University of Minnesota Press, 1973) 98-99.
22. Mimi Reisel Gladstein, *"Steinbeck's Juana: A Women of Worth,"* Steinbeck's Women: Essays in Criticism (1979) 49.

23. Gladstein, *"Steinbeck's Juana: A Women of Worth"* (1979) 50.
24. Gladstein, *"Steinbeck's Juana: A Women of Worth"* (1979) 52.
25. Dr. K. Sreenivasan, *John Steinbeck: A Study of His Novels* (1980) 125.
26. Levidova, *"The Post-War Books of John Steinbeck,"* Soviet Review (1963): 10.
27. Gladstein, *The Indestructible Women in Faulkner, Hemingway and Steinbeck* (1986) 96.
28. Beth Everest, and Judy Weddles, *"The Neglected Rib: Women in East of Eden,"* Steinbeck Quarterly (1988) 22.
29. Richard Peterson, *"The Turning Point: The Pastures of Heaven,"* A Study Guide to Steinbeck (1974) 99.
30. *Ibid.*
31. R.S. Hughes, Beyond *'The Red Pony'* (1987) 35.

III

Domestic Women
Wives and Daughters

Allied to the category of mothers in the class of domestic women who appear in Steinbeck's fiction are wives and daughters. Although they share with the elderly domestic women some of the qualities of the life of love and peace, they are also different from their seniors because of both the fact that they are younger in age and the fact that they have to play different kinds of roles as wives and daughters. Between wives and daughters it is the former who come closer to the mothers for their being married is one of the common factors shared with them. It is, therefore, appropirate to first take up the discussion of Steinbeck's wives who naturally come next to mothers in the general class of domestic women.

Wives

In Steinbeck, an ideal wife is synonymous with housewife, and the wife who deviates from her domestic role is considered either "inferior" or "inadequate." His ideal wives are "domesticity personified."[1] They do not find their job in the house menial or degrading; rather they perform their duty with a sense of pride. They find self-fulfillment in their role as housewives. It is best illustrated by the behaviour of Elizabeth and Rama in *To a God Unknown,* and of Alicia Whiteside in *The Pastures of Heaven*. For Elizabeth,"caring for her child, washing and cooking filled her days. She remembered the time before her marriage only hazily, and with a good deal of contempt." She is satisfied with the responsibility assigned to her. For her, her family is everything; nothing beyond and nothing before exists for her. And to Rama, "cooking, sewing, the bearing of children, housecleaning, seem the most important things in the world; much more important than the things men did." Rama takes pride in her role as a housewife. Her priorities are set by her role in the house. Alicia Whiteside "was glad to leave the domination of her mother and to begin a domestic empire of her own." The outlook of these three women sufficiently proves their acceptance of this life with the role attached to it. Steinbeck's ideal wives prove that the impulse to order and to make of house a home is part of the female heredity.

Steinbeck's ideal wives may be fully contented, confined as they remain to their homes, but their devotion to domesticity does not mean that they play a second fiddle to their menfolk. They are not the subdued or passive ones at home, having no say in the family; rather, they are the creators, the makers of their homes. They rule their knigdom, that is their home, with the stern hands of a ruler. It does not mean that they are cruel; rather, they become cruel or get stern only when the family welfare is at stake or when their authority in the house is challenged. Most of the time, they are the caring mothers to their husbands. They assert their identity in the moments of crisis. They show themselves and their real selves only when the situation so demands. They are the masters at home and command respect and admiration from all.

One of the leading wife figures in Steinbeck's fiction is Elizabeth Wayne, in *To a God Unknown*, a pretty young girl of strong determination. She is one of those rebellious figures of Steinbeck, who are always ready to revolt against the unjust behaviour of their own people. For instance, Elizabeth wants to be a teacher and she makes it against the wishes of her father. Marriage to Joseph Wayne is her own decision in rebellion against her father. And immediately after marriage, she naturally assumes her new responsibilities of housewife: "Elizabeth took on the new life and changed to meet it. For two weeks she went about her new house frowning, peering into everything, and making a list of furniture and utensils to be ordered from Monterey." Elizabeth is a caring wife and minutely looks after the physical needs of her husband. She feels concerned on seeing her husband wetting in the rain. She is worried that he might catch cold. Elizabeth tries to be a perfect counterpart to Joseph. Seeing the sad state of her husband's mind after the destruction or death of oak tree which Joseph identifies with her dead father, Elizabeth does her best to keep her husband worry-free by keeping him busy in this or that activity: "Elizabeth saw how the worry was making Joseph thin, how his eyes were strained and almost white. She tried to find tasks to keep him busy."(p.150). She tries to divert his attention by relating her childhood experiences to him and sometimes by her thrilling activities of the young age. This is one side of the coin. This devoted Elizabeth can become a rebel also, can defy her husband in anger. And that is what she does when she decides on having a ride at her very advanced stage of pregnancy in defiance of her husband's instructions. Her natural desire is to assert her own identity; and when she feels ignored or neglected, she makes him feel her presence by doing something unusual. But Elizabeth is not an imbalanced wife of Steinbeck, who would assert herself at the cost of harmony in the home. She is not an egotist who would give priority to her self-respect at the risk of marital discord. She is balanced. That's why she prepares for Joseph's return, after her momentary revolt, with the same old enthusiasm: "She stood up then, reassured and comforted. And as she strolled down the hill she picked an armful of the late flowers to decorate the house against Joseph's return."

Elizabeth possesses the sharp, intuitive powers of all Steinbeckian characters. She intuitively knows the extra-ordinary spiritual instincts of her husband. She sees Jesus in her man. She finds her husband's hand resting on her head in a kind of benediction. As all Steinbeck's women have the capacity of sensing evil beforehand, she has the premonition of death or perhaps of some mishap in the Glade: "She looked quickly at the rock and saw that its shape was as evil as a crouched animal and as gross as a shaggy goat."

Bearing children is something precious, a very significant event in the life of women. It is a stage when the whole store of mysterious knowledge opens up to a Women. Elizabeth, who is unable to understand her husband's mysterious behaviour earlier, comes to know him at her stage of pregnancy: "And for the first time she saw into her husband's mind; all in a second she saw the shapes of his thoughts, and he knew that she saw them . . . . She stroked his hair and smiled her wise smile, 'you should have let me see before.' And then she said, 'But likely I hadn't proper eyes before.'" Elizabeth's wisdom puzzles even Joseph. She is a sustaining force, a giver of life, a perpetuator of the race. She is like rain that gives life and fades away; she dies shortly after Joseph's son is born. Lester Jay Marks says: "Rama and Elizabeth ...are alike ... as wise wand archetypal mothers and wives. Their religion is inextricable from their femaleness and from their function as perpetuators of the race."[2].

Selflessness is one of the significant characteristics of Steinbeck's ideal wives. Their selfless endurance is admirable. Alicia Whiteside, an example of selfless love, in *The Pastures of Heaven* shares the dynastic dream of her husband. She prepares herself for the role of a preserver of the Whiteside dynasty but her first birth nearly kills her and the doctor declares: "'have another child and you won't have any wife." She knows the inside heart of her husband, his desire for more children. Her devotion to her husband crosses all limits when she insists on having another child in spite of the repeated warnings of the doctor. At great risk to her own life she wishes to fulfill the desire of her husband. She declares, to convince him, " 'women know more about themselves than doctors do.' " Observing the unshakeable strength of Alicia, Richard gives his consent, thinking "It's the grain of deity in women .... Nature has planted this sure knowlede in women in order that the race may increase." Alicia has to pay a very heavy price for her insistence. In the process of having a child, Alicia becomes invalid. Her unbeaten strength is appreciated by the doctor who comments that Alicia posesses the vitality of a monster. Invalidness is not a storm enough to browbeat the energetic Alicia. She maintains her goddess-like position in the home: "And in spite of her weakness, she ordered the house remarkably well ... Alicia from her bed or from her rocking chair, planned everything." Her invalid state does not prevent her from performing her household duties. Nothing could confine her to bed. Her husband recognizes the superiority of her wisdom. Alicia's strength is so great that she outlives her husband for many years to see her husband's wish fulfilled by her daughter-in-law. And when she is assured that the dynasty will be saved, the family, the generation will go on perpetuated by her daughter-in-law, she feels free to die.

Mrs. Willa Whiteside, the daughter-in-law, is no less hospitable and kind than her mother-in-law. Her hospitality is enjoyed by her neighbours: "Her neighbours called her "Willa" and often came in the morning to drink tea in her kitchen." She affectionately deals with Miss Morgan. She makes the frightened Miss Morgan feel comfortable in her home. When Molly is disturbed, like a mother she relieves her of her mental agony. She looks after her as her own daughter: " 'Molly you ought to go to bed ,' Mrs. Whiteside insisted. 'Don't be a little idiot. Shall I have to smack you the way I do Bill to make you go to bed?' " She is a Women of keen perception. She knows the potential of her son. She is wiser than her husband, and more practical, too. She makes her husband understand that their son's potential is different from his father's, so he must not impose himself on Bill. She wants the boy to grow naturally.

Juana, the wife, in The Pearl shares the unbreakable spirit of Ma Joad. Her unbelieveable endurance, her unending devotion to her family and husband is a solid example of Steinbeck's strength-giving women. Juana's strength is recognized and appreciated by her husband, Kino: "Kino had wondered often at the iron in his patient, fragile wife. She, who was obedient and respectful and cheerful and patient, she could arch her back in child pain with hardly a cry. She could stand fatigue and hunger almost better than Kino himself. In the canoe she was like a strong man." She has reached a stage in her relationship with her husband where words become meaningless. They have developed a language of silence between themselves: "They had spoken once, but there is not need for speech if it is only a habit anyway. Kino sighed with satisfaction —and that was conversation."

Though an obedient wife, Juana is not servile. Intuitively she knows the evil embodied in the pearl. Sensing the evil effects of the pearl, she pleads with Kino to destroy it. When he refuses, she tries to throw it back into the water herself. As a 'reward' for her efforts, she gets a hard beating. Defeated in her attempts to dispose of the pearl, she resigns herself to the will of her husband and stands by him in his desperate state of mind: "Juana, in her Women's soul, knew that the mountain would stand while the man broke himself; and the sea would surge while the man drowned in it." Like a mountain, Juana stands and endures, but Kino breaks down and his short-sightedness results in the death of their son. Juana proves herself a perfect counterpart to her husband. When Kino becomes weak, when his determination flags, Juana encourages him, infuses her own strength into him. As Dr. K. Sreenivasan has observed, "But ultimately she won not by opposing him any more but by coming to his aid and succour whenever he neede them most. And her success was owing primarily to her understanding of his nature and also of the nature and significance of their relationship."[3]. She is a living soul full of strength who radiates confidence around. Throughout the novel, Juana remains steadfast, loyal and committed to the family. As a helpmate to Kino, she displays plenty of wisdom and surprising courage. In the canoe she rows like a strong, sturdy man and withstands hunger and displays courage better than Kino himself. Like a mother, she tends Kino when he is wounded, rushes to help him when he is attacked, and drags the body of the man he murdered into the bushes. Again, it is the resourceful, wise Juana who suggests and decides that they must flee. Juana is a strong-willed sustainer. She sustains her husband, and their being together is a hope for their future children.

Mordeen's love and devotion for her husband in *Burning Bright* surpasses even Alicia' selfless sacrifice for her husband. Alicia tries to fulfill the wish of her husband by risking her own life; Mordeen, going a step further, decides to enter into illicit relationship with Victor to present her husband with a child. She is a Women of keen insight who can well gauge the intense desire of her husband. And she is bold enough to use Victor for the purpose. Her love for her husband is so intense, so deep that she can make any sacrifice to bring contentment and satisfaction to her husband. And that is what she tells Victor when he tries to entrap her: "'I want to tell you this,' she said, 'May be I'm telling myself, I will do anything — anything to bring content to him.' " And again talking to Ed Friend she says: " 'I think I would do anything— anything my mind or heart or body can conceive —to give contentment to Joe Saul.' " Mordeen's strong will and determination together with her intense love and deep concern for her husband prompt her to seek Victor's help in fathering a child. Mordeen's selfless act of love makes Warren French and Sandra Beatty compre her with Ma Joad. Both of them find her possessing Ma Joad's determination and strength of character. Mordeen may not be "virtuous" in the traditonal sense of the word, but she finds herself a place beside the ideal wives of Steinbeck by making an unusual, unconventional sacrifice for the happiness of her husband. To bring contentment to Joe Saul, she undergoes great mental and emotional anguish.

Mordeen is a Women of understanding. She understands the feelings of her husband. Hunger for a child is as acute in

Mordeen as in Joe Saul. But in her frustration she cannot think of hurting the feelings of her husband by telling him that he is sterile. She would, at all cost, help her husband to maintain his dignity and manliness : " 'Do you know I would protect him from hurt if I were ripped and burned in the process?' "Mordeen is a Women of practical wisdom. She has the capacity to retionalize a situation. She knows what her potentials are. She declares herself capable of any cheat or lie if that could bring him happiness: " 'Do you know I am capable of any lie or violence —any good or bad that a human can conceive— for his contentment and joy?' "Mordeen first tries to adopt the method of persuation with Victor failing which she ruthlessly uses him for her determined purpose of conceiving.

Mordeen's indestructible courage is at its climax when she threatens Victor of desastrous consequences if he ever tried to disclose the secret to her husband. She is conscious that if Joe Saul comes to know the reality, he would be miserable. She time and again declares: " 'It's Joe Saul's child. I will protect him in this child. I threaten you, Victor.' " And these are not hollow threats that she throws out to Victor; she very well means what she says. She can go to the extent of murdering him to keep her husband's happiness intact. In fact, she would have murdered Victor if Ed Ricketts had not made a timely intervention and taken Victor away from there.

If Mordeen has the potential for such a heinous act as murder, she is also capable of showing perfect love and affection. She tenderly attends to her husband and gives him motherly treatment: "She put her hand on his head affectionately and moved her fingers in his hair." Ed Ricketts pays a tribute to Mordeen for her selfless love for her husband. He has all respect and regard for Mordeen. When Joe Saul comes to know of the reality of the child and the treacherous act of Mordeen, he becomes desperate. Ed Ricketts snubs him and admiring Mordeen's great action he says: "She is giving you a child—yours— to be your own. Her love for you is so great that she could do a thing that was strange and foul to her yet not be dirtied by it. She ringed herself with love and beauty to give you love and beauty. How wrong she must have been to love a fool—and a filthy fool." Ultimately Mordeen's supreme sacrifice is recognized by her husband who accepts the child as his own. Some critics feel that Steinbeck has emhasized the idea of universal brotherhood through this novel.

In *The Moon Is Down*, Molly Morden's love for her husband is not endowed with that intensity of sacrifice which Steinbeck's Ma Joad, or Juana, or Elizabeth or Mordeen possess, but she is the model of the novelist's sustaining women. She is an humble school-teacher, fully contented and happy with her husband and family-life. Her husband is killed by the German forces that have occupied their country. She becomes lonely after the death of her husband. But she is so kind and forgiving that she cannot think of avenging her husband's death. On the contrary, she is so considerate and understanding that she treats most humanely Lieutenant Tonder, who is homesick and is as lonely as Molly herself. Later, Molly is forced to murder him as demanded by his countrymen. Through this murder she not only avenges the murder of her husband but also undermines the Nazi stronghold in the town. That way, her selflessness is more admirable than Mordeen's as her act involves the welfare, the betterment of a larger community, i.e., the whole town. As Howard Levant has observed, "the awakening of the resistance is signaled by Molly Morden's murder of Lieutenant Tonder."[4] She is bold enough to pick up a weapon against the occupying forces when the country requires her services. Molly appears in the novel only briefly, but she is a significant character.

Steinbeck's "inferior" or "inadequate" housewives may share some of the attributes of his ideal wives but they lack the devotion and intensity of sacrifice which the latter possess. They suffer from some aberration in their characters. Curley's wife in *Of Mice and Men* lacks the practical wisdom of Ma Joad or Juana. She is devoid of the devotion of Mordeen. Frustrated in her ambition of becoming a stage artist, and being a neglected person after marriage, she is unable to distinguish between right and wrong. She is dissatisfied with her husband and home. She longs for companionship denied to her by her husband. And in her loneliness, she searches the bunk houses for companionship. A tactless Women, caught between two worlds—the real world and the dreamland—is responsible for her own doom. Her selfishness, fails to bring happiness either to herself or to her husband or to the people around. She is impulsive. Instead of cotrolling her dreams, she allows them to control her. And as a result, she is destroyed ultimately. Curley's wife's presence in the novel provides a contrast to the menfolk. The novelist uses her to counterpoint the male figures as also to expose their weaknesses. Her existence in the novel also helps to intensify the loneliness of the farm labourers.

Jelka in "*The Murder*" is a dutiful wife, though silent and aloof, always alert to the needs of her husband. But she lacks that intensity, that warmth, that feeling of involvement, that natural affection, that spontaneity which Steinbeck's ideal or perfect wives possess. There is no feeling of companionship between the husband and the wife. She is not a perfect counterpart to her husband as there is big cultural as well as communicational gap between them. As says Robert M. Benton:

"Jelka proves to be a quiet, efficient housekeeper but not a companion."[5] This lack of communication between the two leads to her husbands' weekly visits to whorehouses to get his physical needs fulfilled. Jelka's lack of communication, her failure to establish a physical and mental contact with her husband result from her different clutural background. She comes of a community where women know of any physical contact with men only in the form of beatings. Jelka misses that contact here in the company of Jim. As says Peter Lisca: "Jelka becomes a loving and faithful wife only after her husband follows his father-in-law's advice and beats her with a whip."[6] Jelka's deficiency as wife is only unintentional. Her inadequacies are beyond her control. She is victim of her cultural background.

In "*The Chrysanthemums*" Elisa Allen's inadequacies are the result of her egotism. She is not one of those self-effacing women of Steinbeck who are the models of supreme sacrifice. She is strong and possesses the practical wisdom of Steinbeck's ideal wives. She is so energetic that she does not find a proper channelization of her energies in the limited role of a rancher's wife. She finds an outlet of her energy in her fondness for plants especially Chrysanthemums which she nourishes as she would do her own babies. She works a lot on them and is intensely in love with them. But still this is not sufficient to absorb all her energy and vitality and she remains dissatisfied. She has a longing for something—something more than "human nature's daily food."[7] She wishes to escape to a world of wider experience which she could have in the shape of a child but, unfortunately, she remians deprived of it: "Denied a child, a wider world of experience, and that projection of oneself into the world of fresh and broad experiences which possessing a child fosters, she finds a substitue in her flowers, though she yearns for something more."[8] This urge of Elisa for something more makes her feel attracted to the romantic life of the tinker. For some time she wishes to experience the life of the tinker. But that is only a temporary phase. Soon she comes to readjust herself to the realities of the world. Forgetting the betrayal of the tinker who had thrown away the sprouts given by her, she settles down in her married life. She weeps and cries at the end of the story; her tears are as much of self-punishment as they are of self-purification.

Childlessness may be one of the reasons causing her frustration, but there are certainly other factors, too, which contribute to Elisa's frustration. One of these is insufficient recognition of her talents, her potentials and her wisdom by her husband, Henri. Henri fails to appreciate the sophistication and aesthetic taste of Elisa which results in her ultimate frustration. Some critics consider Elisa's yearning as sexual, and others feel that her yearning for "something more" is her desire for 'parenthood'. But whatever it is, Elisa, like Jelka, Tom Joad, and Rose of Sharon comes to face the reality and transcends self by overcoming her vengeance and bitterness for the tinker. Elisa is one of those female figures of Steinbeck who come to recognize their weaknesses and express their eagerness to remove their shortcomings.

Like Elisa Allen, Mary Teller, too, in "*The White Quail*" mothers a garden and identifies herself first with her garden and then with a white quail. But quite unlike Elisa, she does it at the cost of her husband. She is an example of rigidity and selfcentredness. She is a caricature of the selfish, castrating female. She is a narcissist, a hysterical creature who wants to create a changeless garden. She would marry a man who allows her to create a garden of her own choice and is willing to let it remain unaltered. She finds such a husband in Harry whom she destroys with her self-indulgence. She almost completely wrecks her husband in her effort to create a stable garden. She does not allow her husband to enter her room. She has built a safety wall around herself and her garden. In her garden she would not allow any weeds to grow, and in her own life she would not let anyone touch her, spoiling her frigid virginity. She sacrifies her husband to her lust for security. As Dr. Sreenivasan says, "Mary Teller is an example of frigidity and self-centredness of a Women too much inside her own shell. Her demanding nature and exclusiveness drive her husband mad with a sense of loneliness."[9] Mary's identification with the white quail, which comes to drink water at her garden's pool, is an indication of her isolation from society and from her husband. One day a cat suddenly appears in the garden threatening the life of the white quail. Mary persuades Harry to kill the cat. Harry, in his frustration, deliberately kills the white quail instead, and, thus, symbolically kills his own wife. As Arthur L. Simpson, Jr. Says: "Mary's obsessive dedicatio to her expressive creation leads to two humanly destructive conditions: the increasing subordination of all human and natural values to her creation; and second, to a progressive bifurcation in her personality which renders her unable to live anything like a fully human life.[10] Mary Teller is strong and sturdy but her strength is not positive like Ma Joad's or Juana's; rather, it is destructive and damaging. Her insensitivity to her husband makes the latter feel utterly lonely.

Emma Randall of *"The Harness"* shares the strength and courage of all Steinbeck's perfect wives. She is a good care-taker, a good house manager. She is most of the time sick but tidy. Uncomplainingly, she discharges her household duties. Like Katherine, Emma knows her power over her husband; but unlike her, she makes a wrong use of this power. She so thoroughly dominates her husband that he must escape to whorehouse of San Francisco to relieve himself of the tension. The shoulder harness and the stomach-belt, which he must wear to keep his posture straight, are the symbols of Emma's domination of her husband. Her excessive control over Peter has made him so invalid that even after the death of his wife he keeps wearing the shoulder harness and stomach-belt. As Louis Owens has remarked "While Emma Randall has not tried to create an Edenic garden on the small farm she shares with her husband Peter, she has forced Peter to live within the strictures of an illusion she has willed into being. Peter is Emma's garden, and with the harness and girdle that she forces him to wear, Emma attempts to deny the reality of human imperfection or change."[11] She is as cold and sickly as Mary Teller is. She is one of those female egotists of Steinbeck who try to preserve their ego, their self-respect at the cost of their marital harmony.

Mike's wife in *"The Vigilante"* is another example of a shrewish and domineering Women who makes the life of her husband a living hell. She is thin and petulant, all the time suspicious of her husband's integrity. She is devoid of everything positive. Mr. M.R. Satyanarayan rightly calls her a tyrant. He remarks: "Like Mary Teller and Emma, Mike's wife is a tyrant and is very jealous, even though she herself is sexually incapable of making her husband happy."[12]

Mrs. Malloy and Captain's wife in the *Cannery Row* are hysterical, childless women, who have made the lives of their husbands miserable with their obsessions for this or that. They are lop-sided personalities. With their one-sidedness they create havoc for themselves and for their husbands. Their unhappiness, their misery is all self-created. Mrs. Malloy is obsessed with her false respectability and is adament on putting curtains on a windowless boiler where she lives with her husband. As Warren French has observed, "Mrs. Malloy is overwhelming with a desire for respectability which finally asserts itself as a desire for curtains although there are no windows in the old boiler,... her standards are her master."[13] Instead of keeping restraint over her desires, she lets them rule over her. The ambitious wife of the Captain in the same novel neglects her home and her husband for her political interests. She is an elected member of the Assembly and is out making speeches when the Assembly is not in session, thus, ignoring her domestic duties. Like Emma Randall, she forces her false respectability and compulsive neatness on her husband. The Captain has gone crazy ever since he married this Women. He says of his wife: "My wife is a wonderful Women, ...Most wonderful Women. Ought to of been a man. If she was a man I wouldn't of married her." Captain's wife is an example of 'half male-half female' type of modern American Women who dominates her husband.

Alice Chicoy in *The Wayward Bus*, again a childless Women, is another example of an inadequate wife of Steinbeck. though she is deeply in love with her husband, Juan Chicoy, she lacks that intensity of love for others. Even her love for her husband is purely selfish as she feels insecure without him. She has made her life miserable with the false fear that Juan might leave her. She is also obsessed with the thought of her getting old and unattractive. As William Lawrence Jones has observed, she has an "obsession with trivia."[14] She is more bothered about flies than about the people around her. Her obsession, her self-created misery lead to bad tantrums. She cruelly treats Norma and Pimples and insults them brutally in her anger. She can easily hurt the feelings of others but cannot bear the hurt herself. She is a Women of weak mind who, instead of facing reality, drowns her misery in alcohol. She is the least hospitable Women in Steinbeck's world who cannot sacrifice her comfort—her bedroom and bathroom—even for one night for the stranded passengers. Peter Lisca finds Alice Chicoy representing one of the seven deadly sins: "Alice Chicoy, (Representing one of the seven deadly sins) with her almost constant ill-humour, her vicious attacks on Pimples, her physical outburst of Norma, and her constant (and final) anger at flies clearly represents Wrath."[15] Although not a mythical figure as Lisca portrays her, she does have a lot in her character which can be characterized sinful.

Bernice Pritchard, another wife figure in *The Wayward Bus*, is an egotist. She is a hypocritical prude, a Women of preconceived ideas, especially of sex. She is sexually frigid and has made her husband believe that his sexual desires for her are gross and sordid. She also considers the natural, healthy sexual appetites of others as vulgar. She is a Women who lives by rules and rejects knowledge and experience which do not fit into the pre-modelled framework of her ideas. She is delicate and weak and possesses the craftiness of a weak Women. She successfully controls her husband and daughter by pretending to violent headaches and, thus, extracting from them pity and obedience. As Peter Lisca argues, she is guilty of the sin of Pride: "Bernice Pritchard ... except for Cathy in *East of Eden*, is Steinbeck's most evil Women."[16] She fails on both the fronts as wife and mother.

Madame Orden's lop-sidedness in *The Moon Is Down* makes her unable to go into the depth of things. Her "stuff and nonsense" attitude makes her incapable of realizing the gravity of the situations even when their country has been invaded and the Mayor, her husband, is under house arrest. All she is worried about even in the predicament is the physical appearance of her husband. Her mind is occupied with the idea of proper dressing and grooming of her husband, and her dilemma is whether to serve tea or wine to her 'guests.' She may be a good house manager but is by no means a good companion to her husband. Her knowledge of her husband is limited to the knowledge of his physical needs. She lacks the keen perception of Steinbeck's ideal figures.

Like Madame Orden, Marie Pippin in *The Short Reign of Pippin IV* and Mary Hawley in *The Winter of Our Discontent* move at the surface and do not try to swim into the ocean of the mind. They possess household efficiency and dedication but lack the practical wisdom of Steinbeck's perfect figures. Marie's world is limited to the kitchen and the cleaning of the house. She is bound to her domestic economy. On the other hand, Mary Hawley is a nagging wife who all the time makes her husband conscious of his poverty. M.R. Satyanarayan compares her, with some justification, to Lady Macbeth, who is "willing to risk everything for the sake of more money."[17] She shares her maternal toughness with Ma Joad, but her interests are selfish. By her constant nudging she corrupts Ethan. Summing up her characteristics Nakashima says: "It is true that Mary Hawley is a Women of motherly type, but she can't understand her husband as did Ma Joad and encourage him to succeed in the true sense of the word: instead, her vanity finally leads Ethan to his destruction. Mary and Ma Share a common maternal toughness but the former's concerns are egocentric while the latter's concerns, especially her devotion to her family, are totally selfless."[18] Mary Hawley represents the materialistic attitude of the modern American women for whom the concept of family is losing ground and money is taking forefront place.

All these inferior or imperfect wives pale before Cathy Ames of *East of Eden*, who is much more villainous than any one else. Cathy shares all the attributes of Steinbeck's ideal wives like realism, conviction, practicality and resignation. But Cathy, perhaps possesse by a devil, uses all her knowledge, her wisdom and understanding of her husband to bring about his destruction. Whereas the actions of Steinbeck's inadequate wives are unintentional, Cathy's actions are well-planned. She intentionally and willingly rejects her role of a wife. Cathy meets Adam in a wounded state and immediately comes to recognize his weakness for her. At the moment she needs shelter and security; very easily she exploits Adam's weakness for her which results in their marriage. Her marriage to Adam is the compulsion of her situation. On the very first day of their marriage she puts sleeping pills in Adam's cup of tea and herself goes to share the bed with Charles. Cathy is incredibly destructive. She knows that her husband craves for children. And when she comes to know of her own pregnancy she tries to abort herself intentionally to hurt Adam. However, she does not succeed in her attempt and has to bear the twin children. After delivering the twins, she leaves Adam and enters a whorehouse— her original place from where she had come before her marriage. She leaves Adam a completely shattered and miserable man. She knows the intensity of Adam's love for her and tries to give him the same intensity of hurt. Her treachery and perversion do not stop with her desertion of Adam. When Adam goes to see her in the whorehouse, she intentionally tells Adam that one of the twins is by Charles, thus, making his life as well as the life of innocent child miserable for ever. Joseph Wood Krutch has rightly called Cathy "a figure of pure evil outside the reach of all good human impulses. She was a whore and murderess before she married Adam and she leaves him to become both again."[19] As Saikichi Nakashima has observed, she is a "Women of serpentine wisdom" who "symbolizes original sin through her abandonment of her 'mission' and attempt to induce abortion."[20] Cathy is the sole character in the whole female world of Steinbeck who is against productivity. She is the only Women who spoils the sanctity of bearing children which otherwise remains a sacred activity in Steinbeck.

Cathy's role in the society is no less destructive than her role in the house. She is a murderer who forces her young teacher to commit suicide. In order to become a whore, she burns her parents alive in the house; she tries to murder the whoremaster Edward; then she murders Faye, the madam, who gives her shelter. At a very young age she comes to know that sex is the most disturbing impulse humans have and at the age of twelve she starts experimenting with sex in a most inhumane manner; as madam of the house, she introduces perverted methods of sex-gratification in the whorehouse. She keeps the photographs of the renowned persons of the town in embarassing postures to exploit them. Cathy is an exception in the role of a housewife. Wherever she goes, she brings destruction. She is a good illustration of the fact that women despite their insight, their depth, their knowledge and wisdom can be 'hellishly destructive.' Cathy is a terrible example of 'willed villainy,; opting out for the evil and the negative in a planned, systematic way. Like all other human beings she harbours both the good and the bod, the satan and the angel in her heart but she willfully chooses to eliminate the positive in favour of the negative. And she executes her Satanic designs with force and fierceness making a class of herself in the process.

Thus, wives in Steinbeck can be classified as 'ideal' (wives), 'inferior' (wives) and 'hellishly destructive." They all share the strength and vitality of Steinbeck's mother figures. They all are assertive and maintain their individuality and self-respect. But whereas the ideal wives assert themselves only in the moments of crisis and that also only to meet the unjust behaviour of their parents or husbands or other members of the family, the inferior wives do so only to satisfy their ego. Steinbeck's ideal wives will never think of aserting themselves to the point of marital disharmony. For them, their family remains their first priority. But the inferior wives, though in most cases unintentionally, can go to any extent to satisfy their personal ego. They lack the practical wisdom of Steinbeck's ideal female figures whether mothers or wives. They give priority to their ego, small-self, relegating marital harmony in the background. In Steinbeck, family relations are important and his female figures, therefore, are mainly revealed through their relations, their interactions with other members of the family. Cathy Ames is the sole, but very powerful, example of 'hellishly destructive' female figures of Steinbeck.

II

Daughters

Among the younger women in Steinbeck, besides the wives, there are daughters. As wives are shown largely in relation to their husbands, daughters in Steinbeck are shown largely in relation to their mothers. Although both wives and daughters are generally domestic women doing their respective roles in the houses, most of their activities in Steinbeck in the case of wives are confined to their husbands, and in case of the daughters to their parents, particularly mothers. Daughters in Steinbeck are unmarried as well as married: the former being obviously larger in number.

Mother-daughter relationship is of great significance in Steinbeck's fiction. Mothers in their role of perpetuators and initiators transmit their courage to their daughters, thus making them their true representatives. It is like transferring responsibility, passing over the torch to their future generations. They are prepared by their mothers to assume responsibility and position as mother. For instance, in *Grapes of Wrath* Rose of Sharon, originally a selfish young girl, finally emerges as an extension of Ma. In the beginning, her sole concern is the happiness of her husband and herself. She is pregnant and all her thoughts are centred on her baby; she can think only in terms of reproduction and motherhood. Though an obedient and duty-conscious girl like Ma Joad, she lacks the practical wisdom and sharp intelligence of her mother. She is a romantic dreamer who dreams of a bright future in California—a good house to live in, fine job for her husband, and a doctor for her baby. This selfish and self-indulgent girl is slowly initiated into small acts of kindness by Ma Joad:

> Ma said: "Rosasharn, like a good girl go lay down with Granma. She needs somebody now. She's knowin', now." Rose of Sharon got to her feet an walked to the mattress and lay beside the old Women, and the murmur of their soft voices drifted to the fire. Rose of Sharon and Granma whispered together on the mattress.

Later, Ma makes Rose of Sharon fan the sick Granma, thus making her serve the suffering humanity.

Rose of Sharon's real training starts when Connie deserts her. Her own pain of loneliness enables her to feel the pain of others. But the proper channelization of her feelings comes through Ma Joad. After the desertion of Connie, Rosasharn is depressed. Here, Ma Joad offers her daughter a pair of gold ear-rings. Symbolically, she passes over the torch of responsibility and position to Rose of Sharon. This is how she prepares her daughter for future responsibilities. Wearing of ear-rings automatically means the piercing of ears. If she wants to use them' she must display her enduring powers to prove herself worthy of assuming Ma's position and responsibility. Slowly, the initially selfish Rose starts coming out of her lonely cell; despite her bad health she helps Ma in washing the dishes. She also offers to pick cotton in the field so as to add to the family income. Finally, she emerges as a symbol of salvation for all mankind by accepting the role of mother for all men; she feeds from her breast a starving and dying old man. In fact, the birth of a still born child comes as a final blow to her and she becomes the earth-mother. Throughout the novel, it is Ma Joad who acts as the nourisher, feeding alike her family as well as the strangers, but in the final scene of the novel, it is Rosasharn who takes her place with Ma Joad and assumes her preservative role. She, in the words of Martin Shockley, "symbolizes the resurrective aspect of Christ."[21] Most critics agree that there is Christian symbolism in the final scene of the novel. Peter Lisca's observation is representative: "The ultimate nourishment is the sharing of oneself, as Rosasharn symbolizes by literally giving of her body ... suggesting a common subject of religious painting— the Madonna nursing her child whom she knows to be the Son of God."[22] In Rose of Sharon, Steinbeck has projected a ray of hope as she becomes the epitome of reproductive principle for all mankind.

As Rose of Sharon is the representative of Ma Joad, Martha is the representative of Rama Wayne. As Rosasharn emerges as the saviour of suffering humanity, Martha emerges as the saviour of whole Wayne clan. Martha, Rama's eldest daughter in *To a God Unknown* has inherited the keen perception of her mother. She is sharp and intelligent and her superiority is recognized by all the younger ones. It is she who first hears Elizabeth's baby cry: "Martha wore a secret look. She cautioned the others to silence in a whisper. They heard three faint smacks, and instantly Martha cried, 'I hear it.' And even a little after, they all heard the baby cry. They stood in awe, looking at Martha." She has imbibed this practical wisdom from her mother. Martha's role of preservation and protection is seen when Burton Wayne, along with his family, leaves the valley, placing all in a mood of despair and despondency. The children are hanging around their sad parents. At this crucial moment Martha's maternal instinct makes her soothe and comfort the miserable kids. Like a resourceful mother, she diverts the attention of kids: "Martha said, 'Our dog had puppies last night,' and they all ran to see the dog, which hadn't had puppies at all." Like Rose of Sharon, Martha would take her place with Rama in future. Now all children naturally recognize a mother in Rama; there is no doubt that in due course Martha is going to be a future mother to them all.

Rosy in *"The Flight"* is another daughter figure of Steinbeck, whose preservative role becomes conspicuous from the moment she makes her appearance in the story. Rosy, Mama Torres' daughter, is as courageous as her mother. Mama has transferred her wisdom toher young daughter. She is wise and mature. After Pepe's departure to the mountains, Mama cries bitterly and shuts herself in the house, leaving Emilio and Rosy shocked. Suddenly, in the absence of her mother, Rosy grows into a mature girl. Like a mother, she becomes protective to her younger brother, Emilio. Eternal mother as she is Rosy satisfies the queries of her younger brother. On being asked where Pepe is gone, she replies: " 'He has gone on a journey. He will never come back.' " She is a girl of keen perception. Intuitively she knows that this journey would be the end of her brother's life. She knows what the wailing of her mother meant. On being asked by Emilio whether he is dead, she says: " 'He is not dead,' ... 'Not yet." She would come to know of his death from the gestures of her mother. As an extension of Mama Torres, Rosy is a hope for future generation. Like Rose of Sharon, Rosy and Martha are engaged in the task of saving people in their own ways. They possess the love and compassion of Ma Joad. Protection and preservation are their natural instincts.

Like Rose of Sharon, Martha and Rosy, Abra Bacon, too, preserves the suffering humanity despite the fact that there is no Ma Joad, or Rama Wayne or Mama Torres to give right direction to her potentials. In *East of Eden* Steinbeck's insistence is on the fact that both 'good' and 'evil' exist side by side in the human world. Although man grows under a complex of hereditary and environmental forces, he does play through his individual will a vital role in shaping his own character and destiny. This idea is very well illustrated in the novel through the characters of Abra Bacon and Cathy Ames. The seeds of good and bad exist in man; constantly he is caught in "a net of good and evil." Abra, conscious of the bad in herself, tries to be good. She consciously makes efforts to choose a positive role for herself; besides her role as a preservator, she works to preserve Cal from the bad. As against Abra, Cathy Ames, conscious of the good in herself, takes to evil. She willingly chooses the role of a destroyer for herself. Abra, like Rose of Sharon, functions as a redeemer, though there is no Ma Joad for Abra to initiate her into acts of goodness. It is her inherent good judgement which makes her act with responsibility and maturity. Abra is destined to play her redemptive role, so often played by the women of Steinbeck. She possesses the firmness and the tenderness of a Steinbeckian mother: "Her chin was firm and her mouth was as sweet as a flower and very wide and pink." Even as a little girl, she shows the firmness of her mind as she "moved with firm and deliberate steps." She is described as having "wisdom and sweetness in her expression." She becomes a mother to the motherless Aron and treats him like her son. In their game, Abra wants to play his wife but Aron wants her to play his mother—a role so natural with her that she slips into it very easily. Cooing Aron she says: "Come my baby, put your head in Mother's lap. Come, my little son. Mother will hold you." John Ditsky reaffirms it saying that "Abra has been playing a game of the possible ..."[23]

Abra's Womenhood, her motherly instinct, her redeeming powers are all very early recognized by Lee in the novel. He calls the teen-aged Abra "a good Women—a real women." Cal objects to her being called a Women and Lee replies: "A few are women from the moment they're born. Abra has the loveliness of Women, and the courage — and the strength — and the wisdom. She knows things and she accepts things." Like Lee, Beth Everest and Judy Weddles find Abra's Womenness "inherent" and say that she "combines a special wisdom, strength and courage with the loveliness of a true Women, and she becomes almost revered."[24]

Besides wisdom, Abra possesses keen perception and farsightedness. She is deeply in love with Aron and wants to be his wife; so she joins Aron in his momentary religious fervour, knowing that it is only a temporary phase. "Abra followed him. Her feminine mind knew such things were necessary but unimportant." When Aron chooses celibacy, "Abra in her wisdom agreed with him, feeling and hoping that this phase would pass." Abra is able to take a long view of things, for, at the tender age of 14, she is able to foresee the future happenings.

Abra has been picturized as "a straight, strong, fine-breasted Women," whose strength, goodness and warmth have been brought out clearly in the novel in unmistakable words. She is Womenly but her Womenliness is of "bold muscular strength." Devotion, sacrifice, tenderness are part of her nature, but her very features show that she is not weak at all. She is a Women of masculine strength but she does not shy away from her Womenly role. She does not want to be an ethreal being, an angel-Women of Aron's dreams. So she rejects Aron's idealization of herself and refuses to be his "goddess-virgin." She wants to be a normal human being, a biological mother in relationship to a man. She is not a romantic dreamer, but a realist; that is why when Aron joins army and leaves Abra alone, she accepts Cal's proposal for marriage and is ready to be the mother of his children. This relationship is a promise for the defeat of evil. It proves that Cal has the potential to triumph over the sin he commits and live a full life with Abra. Abra is "the redemptive power of a Women, a new wife.[25] The role of Abra's mother in the life of her daughter, in her moral and spiritual devlopment, is almost nil. Whatever positive traits of Womenhood Abra possesses are all either inherent or developed under the right direction of Lee. Lee, in this novel, is the spiritual mother of Abra who recognizes her potential and channelizes it in the right direction.

Ellen Hawley in *The Winter of Our Discontent*, too, like Abra Bacon, functions as a redeemer. She redeems and rehabilitates her father. She becomes his guiding spirit when he is passing through a state of moral chaos. She is just a kid, but sharp and intelligent. He r potential is recognized by her father: "of course I love my daughter, but sometimes she frightens me for she seems to have been born clever, at once jealous and loving." Even as a child she possesses the motherly instinct which indicates her future nurturing powers. As Abra nourishes Aron, her future husband, Ellen nourishes the talisman, the "magic-mound" of the house. "My sleeping daughter had the magic mound in her hands, caressing it with her fingers, petting it as though it were alive." At one stage the father fears that the child may destroy the piece but later he says: "now I saw that it was mother, lover, child , in her hands." He can easily recognize the motherly instinct in his daughter. He finds Ellen not a young child but a Women, for "she did not walk like a child but like a fulfilled Women." Ellen is expected to be a light-bearer, "the new light bringer,"because only she "represents staunch moral qualities of the past. Not only is she comparatively mature and thoughtful, but she is honest as well. Her love of the family's talisman ... indicates her sensitive awareness of the family's past."[26]

Ellen is an individual who reflects cheerfulness, thoughtfulness, maturity, love, responsibility, and a great depth of understanding:

> Ellen brought a surge of pleasure. She will be pretty, prettier even than her mother, ... Her moods, her cruelities, her nervousness are the ingredients of a being quite beautiful and dear. I know, because I saw her standing in her sleep, holdin the pink talisman to her little breast and looking a Women fulfilled.
>
> And as the talisman was important and is still to me, so it is to Ellen. Maybe it is Ellen who will carry and pass on whatever is important in me.

Mr. Hawley is right, as it is Ellen who finally emerges as the spiritual harbinger of Mr. Hawley. It is she who prevents him from committing suicide and, thus, helps him in reestablishing himself in life. Ellen's "higher and purer innocence,"[27] her deep, unselfish love make her symbol of purity and faith. "His daughter appears to him the symbol of honesty, the true inheritor of the light-bearing talisman."[28] It is the daughter and not the wife who comes to know of Mr. Hawley's suicidal plans. First, she insists on going with him, failing which, she puts the talisman, the saviour of the family, secretly in his pocket. To quote from the novel:

> "Take me with you. You're not coming back . . . She grappled me again, and her hands caressed and stroked my arms, my sides, dug her balled fists into my side pockets so that I was afraid she might find the razor blades. She was always a caressing girl, a stroking girl, and a surprising girl."

Surprisingly, she saves her father, thus, symbolically, becoming the saviour of humanity itself. Mr. Hawley comes back to hand over the torch—the talisman—to its real owner. She is the one who will bear the light, the torch forward: "I had to get back — had to return the talisman to its new owner. Else another light might go out."

Ellen is the only promise of the future. She is the only uncorrupt child among the world of the corrupt. Her honesty, her morality, her instincts of protection and preservation are seen when she exposes the dishonesty of her brother who has won an essay competition through unfair means. She writes a letter to the authorities and, thus, saves her brother from future corruption. In Ellen Steinbeck has projected the hope for future, the saviour of the American society, its values and morality. Commenting on her character, Sunita Jain writes: "In Ellen, Steinbeck has given Ma Joad as well as Rosasharn. Ellen becomes the life-force. And she is made to suffer like Jim Casy, Tom Joad and Adam Trask and Caleb. But in suffering they all found not hate, but love for this world where the eaters as well as the eaten are eaten eventually."[29]

Like Ma Joad and all other ideal mother figures of Steinbeck, the Hamiltons in *East of Eden* have stamped their children, especially the daughters, with all the best possible in life. Their five daughters have inherited the courage and the practical wisdom of their mother, Liza Hamilton, and the intellectual sharpness of their father. All of them come up to be as bright as their parents. The eldest of these Una Hamilton, is a thoughful, studious, dark girl. She has imbibed the intellectual spirit and sensitivity of her father. Her only interest is reading books. Even as a small child, she shares secret books with her father and discusses the things privately: "Of all her daughters Una was Samuel's greatest joy. Even as a little girl she hungered for learning as a child does for cookies in the late afternoon. Una and her father had a conspiracy about learning—secret books were borrowed and read and their secrets communicated privately." Una never craves for money or physical comfort; her only lust is for reading. Herself an extraordinary Women, she marries an extraordinary man—a man of science, an intelligent and bright man, though very poor: "She met and married an intense dark man—a man whose fingers were stained with chemicals, mostly silver nitrate. He was one of those men who live in poverty." But after marriage, Una loses her sole companion, her father. Her husband moves away to a remote place to continue with his experiments. Anderson is very much like Samuel Hamilton, but he lacks Samuel's talent for communication. He cannot meet Una at the level her father used to. But she never grumbles, never complains to her parents of her miserable state of mind. She possesses the untiring enduracne of all Steinbeckian women. She suffers silently and catches some incurable disease and ultimately dies in silence: "Una wrote letters without joy but also without self-pity. She was well and she hoped the family was well. Her husband was near to his discovery. And then she died and her body was shipped home." Samuel knows in his heart of hearts that Una dies because of her loneliness: "But Samuel thought and mourned in the thought that the accident was pain and depair." Samuel holds himself responsible for Una's death. Her death leaves him a sad and lonely old man. Una lacks the practical wisdom of her mother. She cannot maintain a balance between her world of mind and the world of boby. She concentrates on the former relegating the latter to the background, and suffers terribly in the process.

Olive Hamilton, the second daughter, finds her prototype in Liza Hamilton. She is very much like her mother, a Women of firm mind and strong determination. She is an intellectual, but not as bright as her father: "Olive had not her father's brilliance, but she did have a sense of fun, together with her mother's strong and undeviating will." Her physical features are indicative of her firmness and pleasing personality. "She had her mother's firm chin and button nose and her father's fine eyes. She was the most definite of any of the Hamiltons except her mother." Like all other young minds of Steinbeck she has an urge for marriage. She is a respectable teacher and wants to marry a man who is settled in a town. She does not want to become the wife of a rancher and lead a lonely, segregated life. So she chooses a young businessman for her husband who is settled in King City. All Steinbeck's characters are shown caught in the constant struggle between the demands of the mind and the demands of the body. Olive, like her mother but very unlike her elder sister Una, keeps a balance between the two and proves herself a successful daughter, a successful teacher, a successful wife, and a successful mother.

Devotion is a natural instinct with Olive Hamilton. She is fully devoted to her profession of teaching. She handles her indisciplined pupils tactfully, successfully avoiding the use of force. She is a hard task-master generally. She has a mother-like devotion and affection for her pupils. She looks after them and attends on them as a mother would attend to her sick children.

She is not only a devoted mother-teacher in the school, but a devoted mother-teacher at home also. A hard task-master and a strict disciplinarian like her mother, she stamps her three daughters and one son with the same courage and strength which she herself possesses: "She was loving and firm with her family, three girls and me, trained us to houseworks, dish-washing clothes washing and manners. When angered she had a terrible eye which could blanch the skin off a bad child as easily as if he were a boiled almond." Like her mother, she is a Women of fixed values. Things never change for her: "Debt was an ugly word and an ugly concept to Olive. A bill unpaid past the fifteenth of the month was a debt. The word had connotations of dirt and slovenliness and dishonour." But in matters of religion, she has not inherited the rigidity of her mother. Her beliefs are drawn from a wide range of sources. Her faith comes by easily: "Her religion is essentially of her own design she does not hesitate to look outside the confines of one set of beliefs or teachings to find the answers she wants."[30]

The third daughter of the Hamiltons, Dessie Hamilton, a gay and cheerful young Women, is in the business of dress-designing. She is an intellectual like her two sisters, Olive and Una, but a light-hearted Women. Dessie "was gay. Laughter lived on her doorsteps." She is the most loved member of the family. Cheerful herself, she keeps everyone around gay and happy: "Dessie was the beloved of the family, Mollie the pretty kitten, Olive the strong-headed, Una with clouds on her head, all were loved, but Dessie was the warm beloved. Hers was the twinkle and the laughter infectious as chickenpox, and hers the gaiety that coloured a day and spread to people so that they carried it away with them." Again, "She was the darling, she was the beloved of the family." This cheerful Dessie, a sensitive Women, who cannot think of giving hurt to others is hurt by a man; she is cheated in love. No one knows the details of her love-affair, but what they do know is: "After a year of it the joy was all drained out of Dessie and the laughter had ceased."

Dessie displays lot of endurance and patience. She bears the pain herself. She shares her happiness with all but she suffers alone. She does not take any one in confidence; she does not bother anyone with her mental agony: "The family was worried about Dessie, but what could you do when she would not admit there was anything wrong with her? She did admit to pains in her side, quite fierce but they lasted only a little while and came only at intervals." Dessie possesses the endurance of all Steinbeck women but lacks the courage and indomitability, which his positive female characters usually display The incident of Dessie's defeat in the love-affair leaves her completely broken and shattered. Failure in love makes her sick. She loses interest in her business and escapes to the solitary ranch-life with her brother, Tom. She loses her will to live.

Herself a miserable creature, Dessie becomes a protective mother to Tom, her lonely brother. She is the only one in the whole family who understands Tom. She is sensitive, and so she can understand the loneliness of her brother. She gives her brother a good company, but herself she is a lonely wretch. She lives a lonely life and she dies in loneliness, keeping her secret a secret for ever. Like all positive figures of Steinbeck, she cherishes no ill-will, no feeling of hatred for any one.

The remaining two sisters, Lizzie and Mollie, live on a purely physical plane. They marry early and are happily settled in their families. Unlike Una, Olive and Dessie, their axiom in life is 'Eat, drink and be merry.'

In the *Pastures of Heaven*, Mae Munroe, the pretty young daughter of Mrs. Munroe, is a girl of nineteen who all the time aspires for marriage. She is friendly and soft and likes to have friends. Mae is going to inherit the plumpness of her mother, but definitely she is not an heir to Mrs. Munroe's stupidity. She is not as intelligent as Rose of Sharon or the daughters of Liza Hamilton but she is not stupid either: "Mae's eyes were friendly and candid, not intelligent, but by no means stupid." Like all Steinbeck's unmarried young girls, she is yearning for a good family-life, marriage, husband and children, etc. Undoubtedly, she would prove herself as efficient a housewife as her mother is: "Imperceptibly she would grow to be her mother's double, a good manager, a mother of healthy children, a good wife with no regrets." She is a self-centred Women. She has not been initiated into acts of sacrifice by her mother, as Rose of Sharon is initiated by Ma Joad. She marries Bill Whiteside, the only son of John and Willa Whiteside. And after marriage, without caring for the wishes of her in-laws, she insists on settling down in Monterey, where she has friends to visit and a society of her own taste to move in. The old white-sides are left in the Pastures living with their ambition of seeing their family go on. Like her mother, she is a self-centred egotist who keeps her interests in the forefront.

Mildred Pritchard in *The Wayward Bus* shares the practicality, conviction, and wisdom of all Steinbeck's ideal women. She does not come up to the level of Abra Bacon or Ellen Hawley in whom hopes for future can be held, but she is definitely one of those positive figures who would keep the society as well as the family united. She is in the process of learning, "a soul in Purgatory."[31] Mildred has nothing to inherit from her mother or father. What Lee is to Abra Bacon in the *East of Eden*, Juan Chicoy is to Mildred in *The Wayward Bus* and gives a line of action to her thoughts. He becomes her educator. Mildred is young, ambitious and talented, but her parents fail to see her potential. Her father's assessment of Mildred is: "A husband and a baby would resolve Mildred's political uneasiness. She would then, he said, find her true values." This is how Mildred's parents think of her ambitious plans for future. In her turn, Mildred finds her parents no better than unprotected children: "The two older people because they felt that in some way they were under attack, and

Mildred in a kind of protective sense toward them . . . . She considered them naive and unprotected little children, and to a certain extent she was right about her mother." There is no sense of understanding between the daughter and the parents: "But if there was a chasm between Mildred and her father, there was a great gulf between Mildred and her mother. The Women who had no powerful desires to be satisfied could not ever come close tothe girl who had."

Mildred possesses the sharp, keen intelligence and insight of all Steinbeck's women. She can see through her parents. She knows that her mother is a poser and exposes her in front of everyone: " 'Pull yourself together,' Mildred said harshly. 'I know what you're going to do. You're going to get a headache and punish us. I know you. One of your fake headaches,' she said viciously. 'I'm not going to sit around and see you get away with it' " Uulike her mother, Mildred is a romantic dreamer, a gril of wide interest and strong convictions, with of course a touch of healthy flexibility. Her open-mindedness clearly indicates that she would change, if necessary, in future. She has adaptability and honesty: "Mildred ... Camille Oaks ... have relative self-knowledge, and are honest to themselves and to others."[32]

Mildred is adventurous and wants to see the world, to experience the world independent of her parents: "Now Mildred kept her own counsel, thought her own thoughts, and waited for the time when death, marriage or accident would free her from her parents." She is a rebel and revolts against her parents' orthodoxies. Her pre-marital sexual relationship with Juan is like "throwing off of the crushing family yoke and the inherited inhibitions that have plagued her."[33] Mildred is Steinbeck's young feminist, but she is a great realist.

Clotilde, the daughter of Pippin IV and Marie Pippin, is Steinbeck's young feminist. Unlike her mother, she is wise and intelligent but unsteady. She is romantic dreamer whose ambitions keep on changing every year. She is a girl of varying interests: "At fourteen, Clotilde determined to be a doctor of medicine, at fifteen she wrote a novel entitled *Adieu Ma Vie*, which sold widely and was made into a motion picture ... From the arts, Clotilde went directly into politics. At sixteen and a half she joined the Communists and held the all-time record of sixty-two hours of picketing the Citroen plant." Clotilde is a violent person who works with zeal and enthusiasm, but cannot stick to a thing or a person for a long time. From politics, she suddenly becomes interested in religion. And "Clotilde's subsequent involvement in politics and religion was followed by her symbolic marriage to a white bull in the Bois de Boulogne. Her celebrated affaris of honour, in which she wounded three elderly academicians, and herself received a rapier thrust in the right buttock, caused some comment ..."

All this happens before Clotilde is twenty. At this age, she falls in love with a young American, Ted Johnson. He is the person who enters her life . Clotilde is rescued from utter futility by Ted Johnson: "It was at this time that she fell madly in love with Ted Johnson." In Steinbeck's words: "Clotilde the novelist, the worldly, the communist, the princess, had for the moment ceased to exist. At twenty she stopped into a fifteen years old love affair, all sighs and a full gassy feeling in the stomach . . . . Her love remained, but she found she could breathe again." Her love affair is the first thing she takes seriously in life and "nurtured the pale plant with care." Whatever Clotilde does in life, she does it with full absorption of her mind and body. Now the love affari takes all her time;

she forgets always to make her bed and wash her underthings. Instinct for marriage is as strong in her as in any other adolscent girl of Steinbeck.

Clotilde is practical like Mildred Pritchard and is critical of her father's impractical attitude to life: "He not only wants to be above everything, every human weakness, he wants his family to be too. He wants everybody to be good— and people just aren't good." Clotilde is wise and mature like Abra and Ellen. Her maturity is recognized and appreciated by her father Pippin IV: " 'She matured early,' said Pippin. 'By the time she was eighteen she had lived several lives.' " But though Clotilde is sharp and intelligent and mature, she lacks the direction, the divinity or the sublimity of a Ma Joad. She lacks that depth, devotion and dedication which Steinbeck's ideal daughters possess.

Thus, basically the daughters in Steinbeck are in no way different from the mothers and wives in his fiction. The instinct of motherhood is dominant in almost all the Steinbeckian daughters. Despite their different tastes, different social and cultural backgrounds, their foremost interest remains marriage and children. Though some of them are the free-spirited women of the modrn era, yet desire for marriage is as strong in them as in the obedient, docile daughters of Steinbeck. Like the ideal mothers and wives of Steinbeck, the daughters in him preserve life in their own way. They are generally involved in the task of sustaining and preserving the weak and the desperate. They possess the redemptive powers of their mothers. Devotion and sacrifice are their natural, inherent qualities. Like the ideal mother figures of Steinbeck most daughters in his novels are concerned with the good of the greater number, relegating their own interests to the background. In fact, they are miniature mothers, an epitome of all motherly qualities — preparing themselves for their future roles on a full-fledged scale.

Notes

1. Sandra Beatty, "A Sudy of Female Characterization in Steinbeck's Fiction," (1979) 2.
2. Lester Jay Marks, *Thematic Designs in the Novels of John Steinbeck* (1969) 43.
3. Dr. K. Sreenivasan, *John Steinbeck: A Study of His Novels* (1980) 126
4. Howard Levant, *The Novels of John Steinbeck* (1974) 147.
5. Robert M. Benton, *"Steinbeck's The Long Valley."* A Study Guide to Steinbeck: A Handbook of His Major Works (1974) 78.
6. Peter Lisca, *John Steinbeck: Nature and Myth* (1978) 191.
7. Joseph Warren Beach, *"John Steinbeck: Journeyman Artist,"* Steinbeck and His Critics (1957) 83.
8. Mordecai Marcus, *"The Lost Dream of Sex and Childbirth in The Chrysanthemums,: MFS* (1965) 55.
9. Dr. K. Sreenivasan, John Steinbeck: A Study of His Novels (1980) 54.
10. Arthur L. Simpson, Jr., *" 'The White Quail': A Portrait of An Artist,"* Steinbeck Quarterly V. 3-4, Summer-Fall (1972) 78.
11. Louis Owens, *John Steinbeck's Re-Vision of America* (Athens: The University of Georgia Press, 1985) 116.
12. M.R. Satyanarayan, *John Steinbeck: A Study in the Theme of Compassion* (Hyderabad: Vidyarthi Publications, 1977) 45.
13. Warren French, *John Steinbeck* (1961) 126.
14. William Lawrence Jones, *John Steinbeck as Fabulist* (1973) 24.
15. Peter Lisca, *John Steinbeck: Nature and Myth* (1978) 143-44
16. *Ibid.*, 148.

17. M.R. Satyanarayan, *John Steinbeck: A Study in the Theme of Compassion* (1977) 125.
18. Saikichi Nakashima, *"Steinbeck's Women,"* KAL (1975) 76.
19. Joseph Wood Krutch, "John Steinbeck's Dramatic Tale of Three Generations," **The New York Herald Tribune Book Review** Sept. (1955) 304.
20. Saikichi Nakashima, *"Steinbeck's Women"* (1975) 76.
21. Martin Shockley, *"Christian Symbolism in The Grapes of Wrath,"* College English (1955) rpt. in Agneis McNeill Donohue, ed., *A Casebook on the Grapes of Wrath* (1968) 94.
22. Peter Lisca, *John Steinbeck: Nature and Myth* (1978) 105-106. Also see, Eric W. Earlson's *"Symbolism in The Grapes of Wrath,"* College English (1958) rpt. in *A Casebook on The Grapes of Warth* (1968) 100; Sunita Jain's, *John Steinbeck's Concept of Man* (1979)66; J. Paul Hunter's, *"Steinbeck's Wine of Affirmation in The Grapes of Wrath,"* in Robert Con. Davis, ed., *The Grapes of Wrath: A Collection of Critical Essays* (Englewood Cliffs, N.J.: Prentice-Hall, Inc., 1982) 46.
23. John Ditsky, *Essays on East of Eden*, Steinbeck Monograph Ser. 7 (Muncie, Indiana: Ball State University, 1977) 34.
24. Beth Everest and Judy Weddles, *"The Neglected Rib"* (1988) 22.
25. John Ditsky, *Essays on East of Eden* (1977) 47.
26. Paul McCarthy, John Steinbeck (1980) 130.
27. Warren French, *"Steinbeck's Winter Tale,"* Modern Fiction Studies XI, i Spring (1985) 72.
28. Dr. S.S. Prabhakar Rao, *"The Image of Boobus Americans: A Note on Steinbeck's The Winter of Our Discontent,"* Indian Responses to Steinbeck (1984) 297.
29. Dr. Sunita Jain, *Steinbeck's Concept of Man* (1979) 92.
30. Beth Everest and Judy Weddles, *"The Neglected Rib"* (1988) 18.
31. Peter Lisca, *The Wide World of John Steinbeck* (1958) 238.
32. A. Pepalla, *"Steinbeck's Non-Teleological View of Life,"* Indain Responses to Steinbeck (1984) 48.
33. F.W. Watt, John Steinbeck (1962) 90.

IV

Fallen Women

Another category of women spread fairly wide over the Steinbeckian world is the category of fallen women—women living in the brothels. They have been given as serious a thought, as respectable a place, as sympathetic a treatment by the novelist as women of any other class in his novels. Steinbeck's attitude towards prostitution "as shown in his works is consistently serious and an integral part of his world view as a novelist."[1] The town Women or fallen Women in Steinbeck is a respectable citizen of society; the whorehouse, a place of honour. Here, prostitution is as honourable a profession as any other. The town women are not looked down upon by the novelist; rather, they are protrayed respectfully and sympathetically, so much so that "whores, pimps, gamblers, and sons of bitches" appear as "saints and angels and martyrs and holy men."[2] The novelist, thus, does not take a harsh view of these town women; they are not considered inferior to the women living in homes. Right from his first novel *Cup of Gold,* as Benson has observed, the novelist stresses the fact that "prostitutes may be fine people who honourably provide a valuable service, and this unconventional idea recurs in later works, most notably with the story of the Lopez Sisters in *The Pastures of Heaven* and the treatment of Dora and her girls in the *Cannery Row*."[3] In Steinbeck, at some places, the brothel becomes a substitue for the family, and the madams living in them, a substitute for the guardians or sheltering mothers. Of course, thes women are no substitutes for the ideal mothers and wives, nor is the brothel-house a replacement of the happy home. But the brothel-house and its unhabitants do seem to receive a moe favourable treament in Steinbeck than do the disturbed homes and broken families.

Steinbeck's unconventional attitude towards prostitution touches its highest point when he describes the function of a whorehouse as similar to that of a church. He contends that both—the church and the whorehouse— perform the function of serving man in his disconsolate state of mind and, thus, helping him out of that frustrated state at least for a while. In his *East of Eden* he says: "The church and the whorehouse arrived in the Far West simultaneously. And each would have been horrified to think it was a different facet of the same thing. But certainly they were both intended to accomplish the same things: the singing, the devotion, the poetry of the churches took a man out of his bleakness for a time, and so did the brothels." The whorehouses here are found performing a verey positive role in the soical set-up. These are whorehouses not in the conventional sense of the word, but a type of houses where service to humanity is given top priority. For example, Dora Flood in the *Cannery Row* sends her girls in shifts to attend to the sick persons when an epidemic spreads out in the town. Her girls would not only sit with the patients but also serve them with nutritious soups. The madams of these houses are known for their philanthropic nature: "There is something very attractive to men about a madam. She combines the brains of a businessman, the toughness of a prize-fighter, the warmth of a companion, the humour of a tragedian. Myths collect round her, and, oddly enough, not voluptuous myths. The stories remembered and repeated about a madam cover every field but the bedroom. Remembering, her old customers picture her as philanthropist, medical authority, bouncer and poetess of the bodily emotions without being involved with them" and the girls working under the guidance of these women continue to be as decent as their madams, sometimes even better than the girls living in homes.

The whorehouses in Steinbeck may better be called the homes for the destitutes; the madams the protective mothers. Here the girls are trained for their life after marriage. For instance, Fauna; the match-maker, in the *Sweet Thursday* would make her girls take lessons in table-manners and postures to acquire a lady-like looks and get married if a suitable match is found. In Steinbeck, a whorehouse is like a finishing school for the girls working there. It is a house for the infirm and the old, too. The girls who are incapable of business and cannot earn money for the house are not turned out, but are given the same comfort, the same protection, and the same affection which they used to get earlier. Steinbeck portrays these whorehouses as homes away from home and the madams as motherly sorts who look into the needs of those who visit them as well as of those living with them.

Steinbeck is primarily a writer committed to the larger issues of society and not to individual problems. A realist and a naturalist as he is, he mainly draws on the social aspect of the characters of these town women. A close study of his novels makes it clear that he has little interest in the erotic or sex aspect of the lives of these women. He seems to be more concerned about their social role. He treats them as social units; in their social role they are shown valuable human beings: "They are idealized mythical, exotic figures that have a position in the public mind."[4] Steinbeck is unlike the modernist writers in whose works man is viewed as an alienated individual facing his destiny in the existential void. A realist to the core, he never separates the individual from the society; on the contrary, he always places and views man in the context of society. He considers man basically a social being and lays stress on the social aspects of his characters.

Some critics feel that Steinbeck's repeated portrayal of whorehouses and prostitutes in his novels as honourable indicates his contempt against false respectability and hypocrisy. As Warren French says," He is simply using the prostitutes to emphasize his scorn of thoughtless respectability and to condemn the making of judgements on the basis of superficial categories."[5] Robert E. Morsberger echoes the same thought when he stresses that Steinbeck perhaps uses prostitution "as a focus for satire, both against puritan prudery and the work ethic and against the hypocrisy of sanctimonious politicians and businessmen who are just as earger customers as the proletariat they put down for immoral habits."[6] Whatever may have been Steinbeck's purpose in portraying these town women as respectable citizens of society, one thing that emerges very clearly is that they are an integral part of the web and texture of Steinbeck's novels and are no less important than other women.

Broadly this class of women falls into two categories: the old and the young. The only exception Cathy Ames does not fall in either of the two categories. In fact, it sounds better to say that these fallen women—both the old and the young —are the counterparts of mothers and daughters out of home. Denied the opportunities of playing mothers and daugthers in regular homes and societies, they find a substitute role for themselves—

their natural role of mothers and daughters in their whorehouses. They may not be fortunate enough to enjoy the respectability of daughters, wives or mothers in the main fabric of society, their roles in the perepheral places like the whorehouses is neither very different from those nor less significant. There being significant difference between the two categories of these town women, not merely on the basis of age but also because of their behaviour pattern, they deserve separate treatment.

The Old

As explained earlier, in Steinbeck's world whoredom is not a sin. His town women do not entertain any sense of shame about their work; rather, they even take pride in their position, in their profession. For instance, Coeur de Gris's mother in *Cup of Gold* is "proud of her position, proud that her callers are the best people in the port. And it pleases her that although she is nearly forty, she can more than compete with the young, unseasoned squabes who come in every year." Equally proud of his mother's profession is the son, Coeur de Gris, who very proudly introduces his family to Captain Morgan by declaring, "My mother is one of the free women of Goaves." Coeur de Gris sees no harm in his mother's continuing with the profession. He gives a further shock to the already scandalized Henry Morgan by showing his approval of the profession even if he and his mother are not in dire need of money. He says, " 'Why should I interfare with what she considers a serious work . . . . Why should I change the gentle course of her ways, even if I could?' " Coeur de Gris is all praise for his mother. He finds her a caring mother, fulfilling the emotional and domestic needs of her son. Her profession does not stop her from mothering her son. Her son declares: " 'She is a dear, lovely Women, and she has been a good mother to me . . . . Ah! she worries so about me when I am off to sea. She is terribly afraid I may be hurt but far more afraid of the tainting of my soul.' " Coeur do Gris takes pride in the faultless, clean ways of her mother's life. he tells Henry Morgan: " 'No Sir, I assure you that her life is immaculate—prayers thrice a day and there is no finer house in all Goaves than hers.' She has been portrayed by the novelist as a good house manager. Like all Steinbeck's women she is a Women of values and morals. The novelist considers her a 'lady'. New versions of Coeur de Gris's mother are found in the later novels of John Steinbeck where occasionally she plays the fairy Godmother.

A madam is to a whorehouse what a mother is to a family. In *Of Mice and Men*, old Susy, motherly sort, converts her place into a refuge for lonely farm labourers. It is a place where the lonesome could for a while get respite from their loneliness. Talking about the place to George, Whit says: " 'Hell of a nice place. Old Susy's a laugh —always cracking jokes.' " With her touch of light humour, Susy tries to provide them with the maximum of entertainment. Susy does not run a degenerated house. Hers is a decent one: "She never talks dirty, neither. Got five girls there." Susy is a businessWomen, but she is not dishonest at all. Though a prostitute, she observers ethics in life. In competition with Clara she does not spoil the sanctity of her place. She insists : " 'My girls is clean; ...'an' there ain't no water in my whisky.' "

Susy possesses the compassion of a mother. She is not businesslike with her clients. She charges a reasonable $2.50, and with the minimum charges she longs to provide them with the maximum comforts. She makes her house an amiable place for the lonely farm labourers. "You can get a shot for two bits. Susy got nice chairs to set in, too. If a guy don't a flop, why he can just set in the chairs and have a couple or three shots and pass the time of day and Susy don't give a damn. She ain't rushin' guys through and kickin'em out if they don't want a flop." Susy gives as much freedom of choice to her clients as a mother would give to her own sons.

Dora Flood in the *Cannery Row* is an improved version of Susy. Madam and girl for fifty years, Dora Flood runs a stern and stately whorehouse, named the Bear Flag Restaurant. As is clear, whores have a special place in Steinbeck's scheme of things, Dora in Monterey is a respectable public servant who is known for her philanthropic and compassionate nature and her Bear Flag is a necessary part of the ecosystem of Cannery Row and Monterey which accomplishes the function of satisfying men's natural needs. Dora's is a "decent, clean, honest, old-fashioned sporting house where a man can take a glass of bear among friends. This is no fly- by night cheap clip-joint, but a sturdy, virtuous club, built, maintained and disciplined by Dora, who, ... has through the exercise of special gifts of tact and honesty, charity and a certain realism, made herself respected by the intelligent, the learned, and the kind." Dora is almost a Steinbeckian mother. She "is a great Women, a great big Women." She possesses the compassion and the toughness of a Steinbeckian mother. She is a strict disciplinarian. She maintains the dignity, the decency of her house: "She keeps an honest, one price house, sells no hard liquour and permits no loud or vulgar talk in her house."

Dora is the conterpart of Ma Joad in the social set-up of

Monterey. She is the custodian of great human values in the Cannery Row. She preserves humanity by keeping the inactive and infirm girls in the house, though from the business point of view they have become totally useless: "Of her girls some are fairly inactive due to age and infirmities, but Dora never puts them aside although, as she says, some of them don't turn three tricks a month but they go right on eating three meals a day." Dora's selfless love of a mother can be seen in the moments of crises. Like Ma Joad she is resourceful and at the same time sacrificing. She sacrifices her own comforts to serve the suffering humanity during the Great Depression: "But during the depression she was hardest hit. In addition to the usual charities, Dora saw the hungry children of Cannery Row and the jobless fathers and the worried women and Dora paid grocery bills right and left for two years and very nearly went broke in the process."

Dora is not only the preserver of human values in the Monterey but she preserves the institutions too by making liberal donations to them for their smooth functioning: "If the police give a dance for their pension fund and everyone else gives a dollar, Dora has to give five dollars. When the Chamber of Commerce improved its gardens, the merchants each gave five dollars but Dora was asked for and gave a hundred. With everything else it is the same, Red Cross, Community Chest, Boy Scouts, Dora's unsung, unpublicized, shameless dirty wages of sin lead the list of donations." Joseph Fontenrose is right in his assessment of Dora Flood when he writes: "Dora's house had the appearance of being a restaurant, Dora had the name of madame, keeper of a house of sin, but was really a kind-hearted philanthropist."[7]

The business of prostitution is against law but there is no

one as law-abiding as Dora Flood. She regularly pays her taxes, and in time, too; she pays her grocery bills, etc., and also maintains the sancity of her house: "Being against the law, at least against its letter, she must be twice as law-abiding as anyone else. There must be no drunks, no fighting, no vulgarity, or they close Dora up." Dora's girls too are the models of decency. They are well-equipped with manners:"Dora's girls are well trained and pleasant. They never speak to a man on the street although he may have been in the night before."

Dora has the knack of an organizer. Very wisely and skillfully she runs her house. She has trained her girls in decency and taught them delicacy. But at the same time she has very systematically harnessed the girls for more strenuous services at the Bear Flag. The Philanthropist Dora, the compassionate mother, the skillful organizer goes out of the way to help the sick, suffering people at Monterey when the infulenza epidemic breaks out. At the moment she herself is facing trouble with her income-tax and the business is booming at the Bear Flag, but Dora sends her girls in shifts to sit with the sick families. Not only this, she even regularly serves the sick with soup from her kitchen: "Dora who was soft as a mouse's belly, could be as hard as carborundum. She went back to the Bear Flag and organized it for service. It was a bad time for her but she did it. The Greek cook made a ten-gallon cauldron of strong soup and kept it full and kept it strong. The girls tried to keep up their business but they went in shifts to sit with the families, and they carried pots of soup when they went." Dora's girls are not wholly absorbed in the business of prostitution; they also discharge their household duties. They are homely. They have the potential to be good housewives. In spite of their business constraints they take interest in activities like the birthdays: "Dora's girls were making him a patchwork quilt, a beautiful thing of silk. ... They worked on it in the late mornings and in the afternoons before the boys from the sardine fleet came in."

As Ma Joad emerges as the natural leader of the family, Dora Flood, along with Doc, becomes the accepted leader of the people of Monterey. Untouchable bums come to her for consultation. They seek her advice when they are in trouble and she helps them out of their miserable plight. Mack and the boys and perhaps the whole of Monterey want to do something nice for Doc but they cannot think of what. Mack goes to Dora for help, to seek her advice in the matter. Dora very wisely suggests a nice party in honour of Doc which makes Mack comment: "Now there is one hell of a Women. No wonder she got to be a madam. There is one hell of a Women." Steinbeck has placed Dora on as high a pedestal as he would place his any other Women. Dora is a decent, kind-hearted Women and a law-abiding citizen in every way. She is an integral part of the whole social set-up of Monterey.

East of Eden is considered Steinbeck's most serious and detailed study in the business of prostitution. Here, we are introduced to gentle, sweet madams like Jennie, Nigger and Faye, along with a wholly evil character, Cathy Ames, who later becomes Kate, a madam in Salinas. Jennie is portrayed as "a good companion, a keeper of secrets, a giver of secret loans." And Nigger, a "handsome, austere Women with snow-white hair and a dark and awful dignity. Her brown eyes, brooding deep in her skull, looked out on an ugly world with philosophic sorrow. She conducted her house like a Cathedral dedicated to a sad but erect Priapus." In contrast to Jennie's and Nigger's place, Faye's place "was the cinnamon-scented kitchen of one's grandmother." In fact, in Salinas, there existed different houses for different moods: "If you wanted a good laugh and a poke in the ribs, you went to Jennie's and got your money's worth." But if you felt sad and lonely and on the verge of tears then "the Long Green was your place. When you came out of there you felt that something pretty stern and important had happened. It was no jump in the hay. The dark beautiful eyes of the Nigger stayed with you for days." Faye's place best suited the "young man puling in puberty, mourning over lost virtue, and aching to lose some more. Faye was the reassurer of misbegotten husbands. Her house took up the slack for frigid wives." Faye's house becomes a shelter, a refuge for the deserted.

Faye is another mother whore of Steinbeck. She has been portrayed by the novelist as the "motherly type, big-breasted, big-hipped and warm. She was a bosom to cry on, a soother and a stroker." Like Dora Flood of *Cannery Row*, Faye is running a decent, clean house where no vulgarity, no indecency is permitted. Everything happens or goes on so naturally and smoothly at Faye's place that no one gets a chance of developing a feeling of guilt or shame: "If any sexual thing happened to you at Faye's you felt it was an accident but forgivable. Her house led the youths of Salinas into the thorny path of sex, in the pinkest, smoothest way." Kind-hearted, helping Faye handles the young boys as a mother would handle her kids and helps them maintain their dignity and confidence.

Faye is a caring mother not to her clients only; she is an equally caring, watchful mother to her girls' too. She goes into minute details of her girls lives and even keeps a regular record of their needs and wants ranging from their dress to their medical examination: "Having a revulsion against disease, she paid for regular inspection of her girls. You had less chance of contracting a difficulty at Faye's than with your Sunday School teacher."

The girls living at Faye's place are the reflection of Faye's personality. As a mother transfers her best to her future heir or daughter, Faye stamps her girls with whatever best she is in possession of: "Just as in a store or on a ranch the employees are images of the boss, so in a whorehouse the girls are very like the madam, partly because she hires that kind and partly because a good madam imprints her personality on the business." Motherly instinct is so powerful in Faye, so natural with her, that within no time she accepts Kate as her daughter. She is so overwhelmed by the love and affection showered by Kate that she fails to recognize the evil in her. Now a mother to Kate, Faye wants her to leave the business of prostitution. Naturally, she would not like her daughter to be a whore: "Gradually a perfectly natural thing happened. Faye, the essence of motherliness, began to think of Kate as her daughter. She felt this in her breast and in her emotions, and her natural morality took hold. She did not want her daughter to be a whore. It was a perfectly reasonable sequence." The mother in Faye is so strong that the caring Kate rouses her longings for a daughter of her own. Gradually, Kate comes to be her accepted daughter and Faye, handing her over the charge of the house, retires to a more relaxed, more duty-free, comfortable life. Innocently, she makes her will in the name of Kate. She fails to see through the cleverness of Kate and, consequently, gets murdered by the wholly evil Cathy Ames.

Faye is not only a careful, watchful mother, but an alert businessWomen, too. She would not give entry to a rogue in her house. She herself is a peace-loving Women and wants to do her business peacefully. When Kate comes to join her house, she intuitively feels that something is wrong with the girl. She does not want to land herself and her house in trouble; so she informs the sheriff about the new entrant: "Faye was not bright, but she was far from stupid. She went to the sheriff and got herself cleared. There was no sense in taking chances. She knew something was wrong about Kate, but if it didn't harm the house it really wasn't Faye's business."

Steinbeck's whores are good figures who wish to help and be helped in turn. They are social animals. Like Dora, Faye also contributes liberally for the welfare of the people of Salinas: "Faye contributed heavily to every charity" and thus "soon became a solid and desirable citizen of the growing town of Salinas." Faye is so gentle that she cannot dream of hurting anyonw and no one could ever want to hurt Faye once he knew her. She is a simple, nice Women and cannot think of cheating or deceiving others. Again, like Dora, she commands respect: "People trusted her and she trusted everyone." Steinbeck treats the oldest profession in his novels with humility and gives a humanitartian touch to his mother whores who are shown to be generous-hearted and charming in their personalities. These women remain happy and contented by bringing happiness and contentment to all those who come into their contact.

Fauna of *Sweet Thursday* replaces Dora Flood of *Cannery Row*. She converts Dora's house for the deserted into a school for the brides. She is more of a public servant than a madam of the house. Her sole aim is "to transform the Bear Flag into a kind of finishing school for girls." A match-maker Fauna is more interested in giving her girls a lady-like look. She is preparing them not for the business of prostitution, but for matrimony: "She makes them girls take table-manner lessons and posture lessons." She is giving them training in etiquettes. She finds marriage "a desirable social condition" and "Fauna's sole aim is to make good marriages for her girls."[8] She puts up a gold star for every marriage. For this intense and instinctive interest in the personal life and ultimate welfare of her girls, Fauna surpasses all Steinbeck's mother-whores.

Unlike Faye, Fauna is a Women of keen insight. When Suzy enters her house she immediately comes to know that she is not one of the kind and is only fit to be a housewife. She dissuades Suzy from entering the house: " 'You don't look like a natural born hustler to me. You ain't lazy. Why don't you get a job?' "She is so sure of herself that she repeatedly comments that Suzy is not meant for the house. Talking to Joseph and Mary Rivas she says: " 'She ain't a good hustler, but when I get through with her she might make somebody a damn fine wife.' " Again she tells Suzy in clear terms: " 'Now I know you'll never make a hustler. What you thinking about, your horoscope?' " She recognizes the streak of a lady in Suzy and tells Doc: " 'She ain't a good hustler because of that streak of lady.' " The moment Suzy enters her house, Fauna starts thinking about her marriage. She is really worried about the girl and is looking out for a chance to get her involved with Doc. She is found doing loud thinking in the novel: " 'I wisht I could stick up a star for that kid. She don't hardly pull her own weight here.' "

Fauna possesses the natural compassion of all Steinbeckian mothers. She knows that Suzy is no good for her business, but even then she admits her in the house only to see her happily settled in married life. Suzy is a liability on Fauna and her house, but her selfless love, her touch of humanity, make her give the deserted girl a shelter. Fauna admits it before Doc that Suzy is no good to her, but she shows her helplessness also saying that she does not have the courage to kick her out: " 'Oh, I can't' said Fauna. " 'She had a tough time. I never had no gift for kicking people out. What I'd like is if she'd pick up an go. She got no future as a floozy.' " Fauna is hopeful that if she does not prove herself a good hustler, she might make someone a good wife.

Fauna takes a lot of personal interest in her girls. She is a comforting, soothing mother to them all. She never lets them have a feeling of despondency Suzy is not very hopeful of getting a good match; she says:" " 'Now that's a bad attitude to take, ... That's the kind of attitude I try to discourage .... I tell you, my girls marry, and marry well!' " She is all hopeful of getting Suzy a good match. She is a friend to her girls; with her friendly attitude she makes the secretive Suzy confide in her. Perhaps for the first time in her life Suzy opens up with Fauna and gives expression to her feelings. Fauna is always encouraging her girls. When Suzy is not confident enough to face Doc, when she is afraid of accepting his dinner invitation, Fauna again comes to her rescue. She makes Suzy confident with her bold advice to remember: " 'You're Suzy and you ain't nobody else but Suzy. Then you got to remember that Suzy is a good thing—a real valuable thing—and there ain't nothing like it in the world. It don't do no harm just to say that to yourself.' " Fauna tells Suzy not to feel inferior to others.

Fauna is a good house manager. She manages things so efficiently and skillfully that she could as well be the chairman of the Board of a large corporation. She runs a neat, clean house and allows no vulgarity there. She is a Women of values. She considers gambling a vice, which is prohibited at her place. She does not permit her girls the use of vulgar and cheap language because "vulgarity gives a hook-shop a bad name." Tactfully and systematically she handles the matters of the house. A strict disciplinarian, Fauna brings to the Bear Flag "the little time of rest and contemplation in the Ready Room after work and before sleep. Grievances were brought out and inspected, quarrels were settled, and all the little matters of interest and despair were turned over and examined for their actual value. The praise or blame were assigned and plans for improvement were laid out with lore and tact learned in other fields. Fauna warped and nudged and bunted her young ladies towards good nature and kindliness, which are the parents of restful sleep." Equally tactfully Fauna handles the matter of Suzy's marriage to Doc. She is sure that Suzy is for Doc. She entraps him, giving him an impression that by inviting Suzy to a dinner party he would be obliging Fauna. She makes him believe that perhaps the incident would arouse Suzy's feelings for a man and she would take up another job like typewriting or telephone operating. She handles the tough Suzy and makes her accept the invitation, though it is Fauna who is going to bear the whole expenses of the dinner party. Fauna is harsh where harshness is required, she is soft where softness can work. She is all ready to sacrifice anything to see Suzy settled in life. A fairy Godmother, Fauna wants to dress up Suzy in the snow-white dress of lovely young bride on the occasion of the party arranged for Doc: "Fauna was one of those rare people who not only have convictions but are quite willing to take responsibility for them. She knew that Doc and Suzy should be together. And since they were too confused, or thoughless, or shy to bring about that happy state, Fauna was prepared to do it for them."

Fauna has stamped her girls with the valuable virtues of love, kindness, affection and sacrifice. All the girls join hands with Fauna in her efforts to settle down Suzy and arrange her marriage with Doc. They offer their best dresses to Suzy for the occasion. Mabel's gesture almost makes you cry when she offers her wedding dress for Suzy:

> Mabel took Fauna aside and spoke to her privately. "My grandma came from the old country," she said when the door of her room was closed. Mabel opened the bottom drawer of her bureau and lifted out a brown paper parcel sealed against air with strips of cellophane tape. "Grandma left it to Mama, and Mama left it to me," she said as she tore the paper. "We ain't none of us needed it." She removed layer after layer of tissue paper and at last spread a dress out on her bed—a wedding dress of sheerest white linen emroidered with sprays of white flowers—stitches so tiny they seemed to grow out of the cloth. The bodice was close fitting and the skirt very full. Mabel opened a box and laid beside the dress a silver wedding crown. "I guess she wouldn't hurt it none," said Mabel. "Tell her not to spill nothing on it. I'll polish up the crown, it's kind of tarnished real silver."

and "Fauna was speechless for once. Her fingers went to the light and lovely fabric. She was a hard Women to break up, but the dress nearly did it." Fauna is a whore with a heart of gold.

Fauna is as respectable a citizen of Monterey as Dora Flood. She is an advisor and a consultant. Her advice is sought on each and every important matter. Practically, the whole of Monterey is bothered about the dresses to be worn for the party. Naturally, Mack and the boys share the same dilemma and are worried. Mack comes to the resorceful Fauna with his problem. Within no time, the wise Fauna solves the problem by converting the party into a masquerade—a kind of a fancy-dress show. Mack is all praise for her and comments: " 'They used to say, if you got something you can't figure out, give it to Mack.

Fauna, it's your dice. You're a bull-bitch idear dame. God te-tum-tum His wonder to perform.' " Fauna is the wise Steinbeckian mother whore whose mere presence brings strength and comfort to all around.

II

The Young

The young whores in Steinbeck share with all the young Steinbeckian girls the ambition or desire for a home of their own. Like all other young girls they yearn for safety, stability and smooth-sailing in life. They have been shown each aspiring for a settled and happy life with a husband and children of her own. Paulette is one such young whore in *Cup of Gold*. Originally, she enters Henry Morgan's house as a maid servant only. Once stationed there, she leads a protective, comfortable life given to her by Henry Morgan in rturn for the wild pleasure he gets from her. Here, she is not a regular prostitute living in a whorehouse, but her life, with all its privileges is worse than that of a regular whore; she does not enjoy that sense of security which other young girls do under the protective guidance of the madams. With the passage of time, Paulette becomes so uses to this comfortable life that she wants to make it a permanent feature of her life. Gradually, however, she falls in love with Henry and longs for safety of a man and a home: "At first Paulette was only grateful to him for bringing her to a lazy, easy life, with comfort and days of little toil, but later she fell frenziedly in love with him." As time pass, Paulette's sense of security turns into fear. All the time she is haunted by the fear of being deserted by Henry Morgan. She starts feeling sure that one day he would leave her and she would be at the mercy of the black men:

> As the year went on, the soil of her love thrust up strong vines of choking fear. She knew that when he finally deserted her she would be far more than just alone. She might be forced to kneel in the field rows and dig about the plants with her fingers as the other women did. And then, one day, she would be led to the hut of a great negro with powerful muscles, and he would bruise her little golden body in his beast's clutch and make her pregnant of a black child—a strong, black child that could toil and strain in the sun when it was grown. This happened to all the other slave women of the island. The half of her mind that was very old shuddered at this thought, and that same old mind knew well that Henry would leave her one day.

Paulette wants to keep him bound to her for ever, which is almost impossible. The only way she can think of doing this is to marry the man. A desire for the secure married life is aroused strongly in her. Now, she starts thinking of the ways of entrapping Henry for marriage because only marriage could bind him to her: "Then, to her child's mind, appeared the doorway for the passage of her fright. If only he would marry her— impossible it seemed, yet stranger things had been— if only he would marry her, then she need never fear." Paulette is so passionately in love with Henry and so passionately does she desire for marriage that she feels jealous of Henry's passionate love for the sea and the ships. She knows that "She must make him love Paulette more than the ships, more than the sea, or anything on earth, so that he would marry her." Although Paulette's desire for marriage is quite natural for a girl of her age, she knows that marriage was not possible for the class of women to which she belongs. She is not a dreamer and knows that Morgan would leave her one day, and that she would be subjected to the fate of a slave again. Steinbeck's characters, particularly the women, may deceive themselves for sometime, but in the long run they show adaptability, and at last come to terms with reality.

In his fiction, Steinbeck has inverted the traditional morality in such a way that prostitution is made to look legitimate and respectable; the people who make an effort to crush it are shown tobe insensitive and inhuman. That is what happens in the case of the Lopez Sisters in *The Pastures of Heaven*. The two sisters, Rose and Maria, do not consider it immoral to give their favours to the customers who buy three or four enchiladas from their restaurant. In a business world, they consider themselves perfectly honest as they never accept "the money of shame." They accept money only for their cooking. The Lopez Sisters are the self-deceiving whores, who "believe that trading sexual favour for the sale of enchiladas is somehow different from selling their bodies directly. They refuse to see themselves the way their customers do—as prostitutes."[9] They have not been painted bad women by Steinbeck.

After the death of their father, the two orphaned but industrious sisters, Rose and Maria, try to make their living by running a Mexican Restaurant and selling the finest enchiladas ever made in the valley. In spite of their hard labour "business did not come with a rush." The day when Maria is away shopping in Monterey, Rose gives herself to a customer, not for money but in gratitude for his eating three enchiladas. Thereafter the two sisters reach the conclusion that "it is necessary to encourage our customers if we are to succeed." Steinbeck gives a touch of humour to the whole situation. The two sisters remain thoroughly religious justifying their actions on religious grounds. After each sin they confess to the Virgin because they would not allow their sins to pile up. They would keep their record straight and clean. As Robert E.Morsberger has rightly remarked, "Steinbeck treats the whole matter as a natural, logical course or events, innocent of any sense of lust or pornography."[10] The two sisters make it a point not to accept money for anything except cooking. And if a man ever treis to offer them 'the money of shame,' they feel humiliated and insulted. But these jovial, self-deceiving sisters stand disillusioned with the society they live in. The Munroes, who cause their disillusionment, are portrayed by the novelist as inhuman and insensitive as they hurt the sisters. The Lopez Sisters face the truth boldly and leave the valley to become regular whores in San Francisco: "The Lopez Sisters, not respected in the Pastures, left the valley to give up their make-believe and accept reality."[11] Instead of feeling sad and desperate when put out of business, rather than starve they close the restaurant and become professional whores. As Mimi Reisel Gladstein puts it: "What Steinbeck seems to be saying is that the two women have the strength to deceive themselves when they can, thus making their prostitution more palatable, but they also face up to harsh reality when they must. Men,in Steinbeck's stories, often collapse when they have to discard their illusions. Adaptability is one of the characteristics that most of his indestructible women, like the Lopez Sisters, share."[12] Steinbeck's objection is against, not the life the sisters are leading, but the ways they have been treated by the society forcing them into becoming bad women. As is generally the case with the young girls of Steinbeck, the Lopez Sisters never intend to become whores. They want to settle down happily in a clean business of running a restaurant. But they are forced to become whores.

Another young whore, Suzy in *Sweet Thursday* joins the profession simply because she thinks that perhaps it might be better than waiting on tables or clerking at 'Five and ten'. She is not meant for the job. As delineated in the novel, she is a lady who is fit to be a housewife. It is recognized by all that she is different from all other whores in the house. Fauna's first spontaneous reaction to her persence is that she is not born a hustler. She openly tells Joseph and Mary that Suzy is fit to be a housewife. She admits it even to Suzy: " 'You wasn't never no hustler, Suzy. At least you wasn't no good at it.' " Joseph and Mary's opinion of Suzy from the viewpoint of business is that "this kid could be pure murder in a hook shop." Even Doc maintains a smiliar view of Suzy. Talking to Fauna, Doc says of her: " 'Somehow I can't see her working at the Bear Flag.' " And Fauna, in her reply, affirms Doc's statement of the girl: " 'Trouble with Suzy is, she's got a streak of lady in her and I don't know how to root it out.' " In Monterey most people agree that Suzy is more than an ordinary hustler.

Suzy is one of those indomitable women of Steinbeck who display great endurance. She remains a model of perseverance. Suzy comes of a broken home; gets married at the age of sixteen, and becomes a vicim of a broken marriage; she loses her expected child. Then, after joining Fauna's whorehouse, she is rejected and humiliated by Doc. ButSuzy is unperturbed. She still has the courage to live on. She knows that a hustler would not be acceptable to Doc, so she leaves the whorehouse and starts living in an old boiler. Through her strong will and determination, she leaves her profession and becomes an assistant to Ella in her restaurant. She converts the old boiler into a fine living house for herself. Suzy is a Women of guts as only she could have the courage of living alone in the boiler.

Suzy has all the characteristics of a good housewife. The old boiler in her hands undergoes complete transformation: "the curving walls were pale blue, and the curtains were stuck to the walls with Duco cement. It was a pleasant feminine apartment .... She had built a dressig table for her mirror and bowl and pitcher, and beside it stood a fruit jar filled with lupines and poppies." She has all the natural instincts of a young girl. First, to marry Doc she leaves her profession; then, she expresses to Fauna her desire for a house of her own. She is happy to call the boiler her house— a place of her own. She is an honest Women. She cannot hide her love for Doc. On learning that Doc has invited her for dinner, "Suzy was restless and unhappy. She felt excitement and nausea at the same time. She wanted to smile and she wanted to cry, and she was scared and happy and hopeless." Her aspiration for marriage and for a man of her own is very clear from her reaction tothe dinner to which Doc invites her. Her strong will brings about positive results in the end. To start with, she is a whore; but by the end of the novel, she is Doc's girl, showing a possibility of future motherhood. She is transformed by Fauna into a girl with courage and conviction.

With the portrayal of Cathy Ames in *East of Eden*, whoredom no longer remains a genial recreation only. She is the black version of the large-hearted whores prominent in Steinbeck's fiction. She is a wholly evil character, a complete opposite of Steinbeck's "Happy-Hookers." Whereas the others are shown shifting from whores to housewives, Cathy turns form a housewife to a whore. She is the only character in Steinbeck's fiction who is an enemy of procreation. She is a depraved prostitute and uses sex as an instrument of torment to express her venom towards the world. She has the potential to be good, but willingly she plays a bad girl.

As wife of Adam Trask and mother of Cal and Aron, Cathy enters the whorehouse of Faye and wins over everyone with her loving, caring and sympathetic attitude:

> Kate put herself out to be pleasant. She helped the other girls keep their rooms clean. She served them when they were sick, listened to their troubles, answered them in matters of love, and as soon as she had some, loaned them money. You couldn't want a better girl. She became best friend to everyone in the house.
>
> There was no trouble Kate would not take, no drudgery she was afraid of, and, in addition, she brought business .... Kate was thoughtful too. She remembered birthdays and always had a present and a cake with candles. Faye realized she had a treasure.

She definitely has a streak of goodness in her, but intentionally she becomes a monster. She is strong and manipulative. From the very beginning she knows her mind and executes her gameplans. She wants to replace Faye as madam, and she easily succeeds. Her task of winning over the hearts of everyone in the house, including Faye, is a sure move in this direction.

Cathy is a good manager. She can manage things efficiently and skillfully to the benefit of the house. With her work she proves that she can manage things better than Faye. Her way of doing things always surprises others:

When Kate offered to help with the marketing and planning of meals Faye was pleased although she didn't know when the girl found time. Well, not only did the food improve, but the grocery bills came down one-third the first month Kate took over. And the laundry—Faye didn't know what Kate said to the man but that bill suddenly dropped twenty-five per cent. Faye didn't see how she ever got along without Kate.

Very tactfully Kate takes charge of things from Faye one by one making her believe that she intends to share her burden. Her plan is to win Faye's confidence, and very successfully she does it with her efficient way of handling things.

Cathy possesses the sharp insight of all Steinbeckian women. As a young girl she comes to realize that sexuality is the most disturbing impulse humans have. Thereafter, she uses sex as an instrument of torture. Her history is one long tale of evil doings. First, she drives her teacher to suicide; she burns her parents alive; she enlists herself as a whore with Mr. Edwards; and then she deserts her husband and children to seek again the freedom of the brothel. That is when she enters the whorehouse of Faye and now she wants to be the madam of that house. With her sharp intelligence she comes to know Faye's weakness for a daughter. As she is a big cheat, she poses to be a daughter to Faye. First, she arouses her compassion by posing to be a motherless child. She exploits the faith and confidence of Faye to the full. So wonderfully does she play the daughter to her that Faye is over-whelmed with her love and affection and makes a will in her name saying: " 'All my worldly goods without exception to Kate Albey because I regard her as my daughter.'" Kate is a shrewd and crooked Women who plans out things meticulouslyand then executes her designs cautiously and systematically. She is in no hurry to grab things once the will has been made in her name. She wants to bring the matter to the notice of everyone present in the house and very cleverly uses Faye to make it a public secret. She makes Faye declare: " 'You see, girls, I'm alone in the world and I have taken Kate as my daughter. She takes such care of me. Get the box, Kate.' And each girl took the will in her own hands and inspected it. It was so simple they could repeat it word for word to the other girls." Now when most impediments have been cleared from her path, and she gets assured that no one would suspect her, Cathy starts poisoning Faye and, thus, clears out the last obstacle in her way of becoming the sole in charge of the house. Rightly observes Warren French that she can "destroy anything that stands in her way, and will scruple nothing to achieve her ends, clever enough to manipulate other people in order to achieve her purposes and responsible for her own destruction."[13]

There is no end to the wickedness and cruelty of the murdress, and seducer, Cathy Ames. She is sadist taking pleasure in the suffering of others. When Adam comes to meet Kate, the madam and the whore, she treats him cruelly and tries to overpower him failing which she discloses the identity of his two sons. She is brazen enough to tell him that one is by Charles Trask, thus, making the life of Adam and Cal a living hell for them both. Adam rightly comments: " 'I' m beginning to think you're a twisted human— or no human at all.' " In the hands of Kate, the protective house of Faye becomes a nasty house. She introduces in that house all perverted methods of sex-gratification. John H. Timmerman rightly sums up Cathy's character: "Cathy's essential evil is indeed the evil of lovelessness: instead of affirming life, she perverts and bends life to her darkness. Steinbeck introduces Cathy as a monster, ... Yet she is and remains a monster for two reasons. First, she bends and twists life. Second, she debases sexuality and in Steinbeck's fiction human sexuality is always a sign of robust vigour and energetic life.... The sexual weapon that Cathy wields wounds everyone in the novel."[14]

Like Cathy Ames, Margie Young Hunt in *The Winter of Our Discontent* is a sophisticated town-bred Women possessed of the repulsive aspects of feminine personality. She is cunning and shrewd like Cathy, but not as destructive as the latter. She makes a puppet of Ethan and initiates him into the world of corruption. Actually, she is a weak Women keeping up a bold face. After the death of her husband she needs a man to depend upon. Thinking that Ethan will be sort of backlog for her, she sets about the task of making Ethan rich. Her cleverness is the result of her feeling of insecurity whereas Cathy is intentionally and willingly a bad Women. Margie Young Hunt is the town's temptress for lonely, lost men. She is Steinbeck's another housewife turning to promiscuity.

In *Tortilla Flat*, the promiscuous group of women, consisting of Mrs. Morale, Cornelia Ruiz, Mrs. Torelli, Dolores Engracia Ramirez, Tia Ignacia, Senora Teresina Cortez and Gracia Montez, has been presented in a gentle, light and humorous tone. Steinbeck is not critical of these women as they are not vicious like Cathy Ames. Rather, like the Lopez Sisters, they are the people in love wih life. Their way of making love shows that they are dynamic, energetic, and vital. They are women living on the level of flesh alone. They are selfish and lack the higher instincts of Steinbeck's positive female figures, but definitely they cannot be linked with the wholly evil or negative characters like Cathy and Margie Young Hunt. The only thing that can be said about them is that they are human beings living on the animal plane, enjoying the baser instincts of life—nothing beyond flesh exists for them.

They are not regular whores living in whorehouses, but are no better than the whores.

Thus, by portraying the fallen women as respectable citizens of society, Steinbeck establishes the point that morality is a matter of arbitrariness. It is only a question of social morality which makes them inferior to others. Otherwise, most of them emerge as superior to the imbalanced women living in regular homes. In fact, their role in society as dipicted by Steinbeck, is no less significant than the role of his ideal figures. These fallen women of Steinbeck are difinitely more superior, more compassionate, more caring for others than his self-centred egotists. That way, they can easily to placed with the ideal figures—mothes or wives or daughters— of Steinbeck. Like Hawthorne, Steinbeck believes that morality is attached to human values. Hawthorne, in *The Scarlet Letter* points out that "to err is human" and the persons tend to be more human after erring. Both Hawthorne and Steinbeck establish that those who err, those who fall, become more understanding of other human beings; they behave at level with the people. They become closer to the common suffering humanity. Undoubtedly, home brings social respectability to a Women,but it brings some restrictions too; whorehoue compensates respectability by bringing more freedom.

NOTES

1. Peter Lisca, *The Wide World of John Steinbeck* (1958) 205.
2. Cannery Row, 273.
3. Jackson J. Benson, *The True Adventures of John Steinbeck* (1984) 116.
4. Charles R. Metzgner, *"Steinbeck's Version of the Pastoral,"* Modern Fiction Studies VI. 2 Summer (1960):118.

5. Warren French, *John Steinbeck* (1961) 179.
6. Robert E. Morsberger, *"Steinbeck's Happy Hookers,"* Steinbeck's Women: Essays in Criticism (1979) 39.
7. Joseph Fontenrose, *John Steinbeck: An Introduction and Interpretation* (1963) 104.
8. Joseph Fontenrose, *John Steinbeck: An Introduction and Interpretation* (1963) 128.
9. R. S. Hughes, Beyond *'The Red Pony'* (1987) 42.
10. Robert E. Morsberger, *"Steinbeck's Happy Hookers"* (1979) 39-40.
11. Joseph Fontenrose, *John Steinbeck: An Introduction and Interpretation* (1963) 26.
12. Mimi Reisel Gladstein, *The Indestructible Women in Faulkner, Hemingway and Steinbeck* (1984) 91.
13. Warren French, *John Steinbeck* (1961) 153.
14. John H. Timmerman, *John Steinbeck's Fiction: The Aesthetics of the Road Taken* (1986) 219-20.

V

Working Women

Working women do find a place in the fictional world of Steinbeck, although they have not been presented as favourably as his domestic women or even the fallen women. They neither abound in number as do the domestic women, nor do they receive as sympathetic a treatment as do the fallen women. It may sound surprising that a novelist having such an untraditional and unconventional attitude towards whores and whoredom should become so traditional and conventional in his depiction of working women. Actually, there is nothing odd or paradoxical here. Whereas his attitude towards the whores is dictated by his humanitarianism, his response to the female professionals seems to have been strongly influenced, even dictated, by the social attitudes of the Depression Era in America. During this period of Great Depression women are mostly shown in their homes playing the role of sustaining their men. If ever they come out of the house, it is only to work as labourers in the fields by the side of their men. Besides, there are teachers who stick to their jobs until they enter their domestic life. This attitude of Steinbeck may encourage one to conclude that although he is not against the idea of women taking to professions alongside men, he seems to consider women basically domestic. The women in his fiction do adopt various professions, particularly the soft ones like teaching or fine arts but they always abandon these professions as soon as they are able to find their life companions.

If Steinbeck's objection against married women taking up careers outside homes had stemmed only from the economic conditions of contemporary America in the 30s, they would have ended with the ending of the Great Depression. But one finds that Steinbeck continues to adhere to the idea of married women moving out of their homes all along his literary career spread over a long period of forty years. A study of the situations in his novels reveals that Steinbeck regards the job of a housewife or a mother a whole time career for a Women—as also a universally accepted first career for a Women anywhere. He seems to believe that the domestic responsibilities demand all the time and energy of a Women. Similarly, he seems to view the other professions outside home equally demanding, which cannot be combined with the responsibilities like that of a mother or a wife. Steinbeck seems to be convinced that an attempt at combining the two can only mean sacrificing one for the other. For instance, the Captain's wife in the *Cannery Row* is a politician. Her interest in politics, her life outside her home, leaves her husband a wretched man and her home a miserable place to live in. She fulfills her political ambitions at the cost of the interests of her husband and her h ome. She sacrifices one at the altar of the other. She is unable to cope with the demands of her political as well as domestic world. Then there is Alice Chicoy in *The Wayward Bus* who is running independently a roadside restaurant. The result of her involvement in the business world is that she becomes a highly frustrated wife. She cannot satisfy her husband and is all the time suspicious of his behaviour. The reason, obviously, is that she cannot handle the two jobs simultaneously and her failure to do so results in her bad temperament. She is neither a good businessWomen nor a good housewife. The two examples clearly indicate that Steinbeck does not want his women to make a mess of both the home and the career by combining the two. He wants his fictional creations to be good housewives or successful professionals. That is why, if a professional gets married in Steinbeck, she ceases to be a professional.

This attitude of Steinbeck towards working women may mislead one to think that the novelist is against the working women. But this is not the case. He may be against the 'radicals'—'half male, half female' type of modern American women—but this prejudice does not mean that he is against the working women. If it had been so, there would not have been in his fiction the emergence of career women as early as in the 30s, almost in the beginning of his career as a novelist. In his second novel, *To a God Unknown,* there appears Elizabeth, an ideal teacher of Steinbeck. Then, again, in his third novel *The Pastures of Heaven*, there emerge Miss Martin and Miss Morgan, the two ideal teachers of Steinbeck, who discharge their duties in the field of teahing almost up to perfection. There is Molly Morden in *The Moon is Down*, who before marriage works as a grammar teacher in a school. And Olive Hamilton, as late as in the 50s, in *East of Eden*, chooses to be a teacher, too. Then there are waitresses like Norma in *The Wayward Bus* and Suzy in Sweet Thursday who skillfully manage the work of the restaurant. Businesswomen, too, find representation in the novels of Steinbeck in the form of Dessie Hamilton in *East of Eden*, Alice Chicoy in *The Wayward Bus*, and Ella in *Sweet Thursday.* Besides teachers, businesswomen and waitresses, we come upon women artists in his novels. Camile Oaks in *The Wayward Bus* and Suzanne in *The Short Reign of Pippin IV* are two such young stage artists, along with a number of others, who wish to emulate their example and become artists but are not able to attain the ideal. To be sure, these women are depicted without any prejudice. In fact, the writer seems to appreciate their talent and capacity to succeed even in the professions otherwise considered suitable for men.

Teachers form a major chunk of the professional group among Steinbeck's women. R.S. Hughes observes: "School teachers are one group of women Steinbeck takes seriously."[1] They are highly respectable citizens of the country. They enjoy good reputation in society. Anyone would welcome to board a teacher in the house as "a family gained social ascendency by boarding the teacher."[2] In Steinbeck a school teacher is considered a person of social as well as educational importance who is supposed to impart an intellectual and cultural tone to her region. Having a teacher in the house is like "having a priest in the family."[3] A teacher in his fictional world is the most admired young Women from the matrimonial point of view, too: "And the teacher was not only an intellectual paragon and a social leader, but also the matrimonial catch of the countryside. A family would indeed walk proudly if a son married the school teacher. Her children were presumed to have intellectual advantages both inherited and conditioned."[4] A tacher attains a dignified position in society; she is not only the custodian of her pupils' and the society's cultural and intellectual growth but also brings "social elevation to a man."[5] In fact, teachrs are the only ones in Steinbeck who have willingely chosen their profession partly because teaching is one of the professions suited to young girls and partly because "school teaching could be, if the teacher wished to make it so, a subtle and certain move towards matrimony."[6] Other professionals in Steinbeck like the artists and the waitresses, are the unwilling entrants in their respective professions. They are the victims of circumstances and take up their jobs under compulsion of their respective situations. The businesswomen like Dessie and Ella, too, seem to have entered the professional field only to get a suitable match for themselves.

One thing commonly shared by all the young working women of Steinbeck is their strong instinct for marriage. For all of them, marriage comes first, profession only later. In fact, in most cases, profession is only a way to matrimony. Being a realist, Steinbeck knows that marriage is an instinct universally shared by all young women. And this is also an established fact that the suppression of natural instincts leads to perversion until and unless these instincts are sublimated. This may be one of the reasons why for all young women of Steinbeck profession is only secondary. Elizabeth, Olive Hamilton and Molly Morden leave their jobs for the sake of marriage. Miss Martin and Miss Morgan are waiting for their chance to come. Suzy leaves the profession of prostitution and becomes a waitress only to win over Doc. Norma leaving her job of a waitress wants to join film line only with an ambition of getting a suitable match. Suzanne, in normal course, would have liked to marry a man of her own choice. Camille Oaks' sincere desire is to hve a home of her own with a husband and two children. Dessie Hamilton, a flourishing businessWomen, falls in love with a man. On being jilted by him, she closes down her business and goes back to her parental ranch house to give company to her lonely brother, Tom.

These working women in Steinbeck are not those radical

feminists who would demand equality with man in every walk of life. They do, however, represent the new women of the post-war period in America, who are certainly different from the traditional housewives of the pre-war American society governed by the quasi-Victorian values of a conservative society. They are freedom-loving, self-reliant women who want to be financially and socially independent. Although they do not adopt high profile of radicalism they do quietly and unselfconsciously demonstrate their disapproval of the traditional image of Women and a clear perference for a life of independence. For instance, Elizabeth McGreggor starts studying for county examinations against the wishes of her father so that she could be a teacher. Again, she joins the profession of teaching in defiance of her father. She is freedom-loving and wants to leave her home to lead an adventurous, unprotected and unguarded life. She marries Joseph Wayne against the wishes of her father. Similarly, Olive Hamilton independently decides a career for herself. She has a strong urge for metropolitan life, so she decides to be a teacher. She chooses a businessman for husband and keeps her engagement a secret from her near and dear ones till the completion of her term in the school. Suzy is another example of the new women of the post-war America. She is a freebird, a bold and courageous Women of guts who chooses to live alone in a boiler. These working women of Steinbeck stand somewhere in between his domestic women and the radical feminists of the post-war America.

Steinbeck's working women, too, posses the determination and devotion of his domestic women. They are as devoted to their various professions as his domestic women are to their families. They are young enthusiasts bubbling with life and showing great interest in their professions. They are all for their professions till they are professionals and they show equal enthusiasm for domestic life when they become housewives and mothers. For instance, Elizabeth McGreggor, a successful teacher, becomes Elizabeth Wayne, a successful and devoted housewife. Similarly, Olive Hamilton, a disciplinarian as teacher, is equally a disiplinarian as mother to her two daughters and one son. Steinbeck's women are for perfection in either field; they are either perfect mothers or perfect career women.

I

Teachers

The first of the professional Women to make her appearance in Steinbeck's fiction is Elizabeth, in *To a God Unknown*, who is a Women of strong will and firm determination. Her physcial features indicate the firmness of her mind. "Elizabeth was a pretty girl, and very determined. Her hair was fluffy, her nose small, and her chin firm from setting it against her father.... She was a tall girl; not thin, but lean with strength and taut with quick and nervous energy." Not only her physical features, but her gestures, her practical actions, too, indicate her rebellious nature. Her revolt is against the unjust and inhuman treatment meted out by her father who is always out to contradict anything said by Elizabeth or her mother. Elizabeth is not at all disrespectful to her father; she does not abuse him, or insult him in the presence of others. But, rather, hers is a silent revolt. She has learnt never to give an outlet to her feelings. She would never let him know what her opinions are: "He tried to browbeat his daughter Elizabeth and failed as miserably as he had with her mother, for Elizabeth set her mouth and held her opinions out of reach of his arguments by never stating them. It infuriated the old man to think that he could not blast her prejudices with his own because he did not know what they were." Elizabeth gives a real shock to her father when she decides on becoming a teacher: " McGreggor was shocked, nevertheless, when Elizabeth began studying for county examinations so she could be a teacher." And then she marries a man of her own choice against the wishes of her father. But all her revolt is against the uncalled for behaviour of her father. She never forgets to pay him his due respect. She shows her willingness to meet her father once before marriage. She tells Joseph: " 'there are a thousand things that must be done. I should go home to Monterey for a little. Of course my father will want to see me once before I am married.' "

Elizabeth is a wise Women of keen intelligence. At a very young age, she comes to know how to handle things, much as how to tackle her assertive father: "In a house where the littlest statement automatically marshalled crushing forces of argument against itself, she had learned to be silent." She is equally wise and sincere in her profession. She is a well-read Women and does justice to her job. She is a teacher who would give priority to the interest of her students. She frankly tells Joseph Wayne that their marriage is possible only at the end of her term. On being asked by Joseph Wayne when they will be married she replies: " 'Why, I must serve out my year.' " Elizabeth remains a good teacher when in job, and good housewife when married. The novelist has not indicated whether Elizabeth has been pressurized by John Wayne to leave the job or it is her own decision. However, it is very clear that leaving the job is not any precondition for marriage set by Mr. Wayne. It seems,one may safely conclude, that Elizabeth on her own decides to leave the job after marriage perhaps feeling that it would be difficult to cope with the contrary demands of home and profession.

Other characters who figure as teachers are Miss Martin and Miss Morgan, the two ideal teachers of Steinbeck in *The Pastures of Heaven*. Miss Martin possesses the sharp perception of Elizabeth but lacks her wisdom. Tularecito, an underdeveloped son of Franklin Gomez, has been coming to school for the last five years showing no sign of progress in any field. Teachers in the Pastures miserably fail to handle the boy. However, soon after her joining the school, Miss Martin takes charge of the boy. She shows deep interest in him and handles him tactfully. She comes to recognize the hidden talent of the boy for drawing pictures. She discovers the genius in him and tries to foster it: "When Miss Martin, the teacher, discovered his ability, she gave him a piece of chalk and told him to make a procession of animals round the blackboard. Tularecito worked long after school was dismissed, and next morning an astounding parade was shown on the walls. All of the animals Tularecito had ever seen were there; all the birds of the hills flew above them." Sincerely and efficiently Miss Martin gives the boy a direction. She finds a constructive way out to channelize the strength and energy of Tularecito. She openly appreciates and encourages him: "Miss Martin was overcome with the genius of Tularecito. She praised him before the class and gave a short lecture about each one of the creatures he had drawn. In her own mind she considered the glory that would come to her for discovering and fostering this genius."

Miss Martin, who could discover the talent of an underdeveloped and channelize it properly, however, fails to recognize that the boy does not possess the wisdom of differentiating between right and wrong. She is unable to notice the fact that the boy completely lacks the power of thinking. She fails to see the animal in him. The boy fights with his hands, feet, teeth and head when the pictures drawn by him are erased by the students of the fourth standard. Tularecito possesses the strength of a mad man and he fights like an animal making all others run away from there. Miss Martin's one unwise step of ordering removal of his drawings creates the whole mess. The boy fights back only in his own defense. He never hurts anyone till he is allowed to draw pictures on the blackboard and his pictures remain undisturbed there. Miss Martin still fails to recognize that the boy is merely an animal who is to be tamed with love and affection. After the incident she goes to the boy's father and wants him to punish the boy for his unruly behaviour. Gomez unwillingly whips the boy severely. And when it is done, the boy, still smiling, goes back to the barn. This comes to Miss Martin as a real shock. Now she realizes that he is no better than an animal:

> Miss Martin had watched the end of the punishment with horror. 'Why, he's an animal,' she cried. 'It was just like whipping a dog.' Franklin Gomez Permitted a slight trace of his contempt for her to show on his face. 'A dog would have cringed.' he said. 'Now you have seen, Miss Martin. You say he is an animal, but surely he is a good animal. You told him to make pictures and then you destroyed his pictures. Tularecito does not like that ....' "

Miss Martin fails to understand certain things. All the time she is haunted by the fear of the incident and, at the end of the term, she resigns her post, giving ill health as her reason. Miss Martin, like Mrs. Munroe in the same novel, is a girl of good intentions but her lack of wisdom, her way of seeing and then doing things always create a mess. Things done by her even with the best of intentions always end in the misery of others. Here it is Tularecito who is beaten by his father only because of Miss Martin.

Teachers in Steinbeck tend to be more idealistic. Miss Morgan who replaces Miss Martin in the school of the Pastures is another ideal figure. She looks upon her profession as a trade which will flourish with her sincere efforts and hard work. Miss Morgan is a young enthusiast who innovates new methods of teaching. She is a teacher who makes school a lovable place: "Miss Morgan enjoyed teaching and made school an exciting place where unusual things happened." Unlike Miss Martin, she is wise. She knows that it is a real hard job to tame the tough boys who are really bigger than herself. But she accomplishes this job efficiently. She sees to it that the classroom teaching is made interesting for them: "The pupils received Miss Morgan's innovations with enthusiasm. Classes became exciting, and even the boys who had made enviable reputations through teacher-baiting, grew less interested in the possible burning of the school house." She introduces a method of reading stories in the afternoon for half an hour. It is a practice which makes her pupils almost adore her. She is a good reader and makes listening an exciting experience for the listeners: "Miss Morgan read well. Even the tougher boys were won over until they never played hookey for fear of missing an instalment until they leaned forward gasping with interest." She, thus, has an intelligent way of handling things and tackles the older children wisely. The community, which was skeptic of the potential of a too young and dangerously pretty Women, Miss Morgan, is now all praise for her.

Miss Morgan is a romantic adventurer. She meets and accepts the challenges of her profession boldly. Like a true businessWomen, she calculates and plans the whole thing before putting her hands into a trade. Before taking up the job as a teacher in the school of Pastures, she studies the whole situation. She takes an assessment of the whole situation she is going to deal with, the type of students she is going to handle, and the type of society she is going to move in. Accordingly, she chalks out the whole plan concerning her future profession. Beforehand she knows both about the existence of Tularecito in the school and the incident of his beating at Miss Martin's instance. Unlike Miss Martin, who proves to be an escapist in her profession, Miss Morgan prepares herself for the challenge of handling Tularecito: "From the first Miss Morgan was vastly impressed with Tularecito. She knows all about him, had read books and taken courses about him." She is highly enthusiastic and innovative in the case of Tularecito. Having heard about the fight, she marks off a border round the top of the blackboard for Tularecito to fill the place with his drawings of animals. When there is no more place left for him to make more drawings, she buys him a huge drawing-board and a soft pencil with her own money. She has found a way to keep him busy with his drawings: "After that he did not bother about spelling. Everyday he laboured over his drawingboard, and every afternoon presented the teacher with a marvellously wrought aninal. She pinned his drawings to the school room wall above the blackboard." The new teacher's patience and her sympathetic treatment of the boy bring about a wonderful change in him. Slowly the boy starts taking interest in her stories. He tries his best to pick up and understand her words: "Now a change came over Tularecito. Gradually, as Miss Morgan read about elves and brownies fairies, pixies, and changelings, his interest centred and his busy pencil lay idly in his hand. Then she read about gnomes, and their lives and habits, and he dropped his pencil altogether and leant towards the teacher to intercept her words." As a result of her sincere efforts, Tularecito starts reacting in a bit normal way. Totally an abnormal child, he is now able to understand what his teacher says of gnomes and elves. Miss Morgan plans a fate for the boy perhaps different from what nature had designed for him. But all her efforts come to nothing when one day Tularecito digs a hole in the garden of Mr. Munroe to search for the gnomes. Mr. Munroe tries to fill the hole and is attacked by the boy who cannot stand that his work should be undone by someone. After the incident, Tularecito is last seen being admitted to an asylum lest he should kill someone.

Miss Morgan is a successful professional, who performs her duties creditably. She faces her professional struggles boldly but in the struggle of life she remains an escapist. She is romantic, living in the world of dreams and illusions. She lives in her own make-believe world. She cherishes sweet memories of her father who is actually a drunkard. She is not ready to accept the ugly facet of her father's life. She fondly hopes that her father, who had not returned home for the last few years, would suddenly come back some day. One day Mr. Munroe in the regular school-board meeting talks of a new man on his ranch. Miss Morgan immediately concludes that the man must be her father and, lest her fears should come true, she resigns her prestigious position in the valley and goes back. Miss Morgan is not a hard core realist like Camille Oaks in *The Wayward Bus* and Suzanne in *The Short Reiign of Pippin IV*. It is painful that so bold a professionist should be so weak a Women in real life.

Another professional who figures among Steinbeck's ideal teachers is Olive Hamilton in *East of Eden*. Olive is young, pretty and determined like Elizabeth. She is bold and courageous. She inherits her toughness of mind and body from her mother, Liza Hamilton, and her love of learning from her father, Samuel Hamilton. At a very early stage in her life, Olive decides to be a teacher and she is successful in the profession even at the age of eighteen: "Olive Hamilton became a teacher. That meant she left home at fifteen and went to live in Salinas, where she could go to secondary school. At seventeen she took county board examinations, which covered all the arts and sciences, and at eighteen she was teaching school at Peach Tree." Olive possesses her mother's strong and unflinching will. She enjoys the freedom of taking decisions about her life. Her life spent in Salinas with her parents has made her decide that she would not be a ranch-wife. She longs for the town life, and the moment she gets a chance she grabs it: "Busy though she was with her teaching, Olive longed for the metropolitan life, and when the young man who had built the flour mill in King City sued properly for her hand, she accepted him subject to a long and secret engagement." Olive displays great courage and wisdom in facing the marriage proposals while in job. To keep her engagement a secret is a necessity for if she makes it know, she is likely to have trouble from the young suitors in the neighbourhood.

Olive is far better read than most of her contemporaries. She has to teach a host of subjects in the school: "She taught reading to the first grade and algebra to the eighth. She led the singing, acted as a critic of literature, wrote the social notes that went weekly to the *Salinas Journal*." She is not only to teach so many subjects but also to teach students of all age groups. It is really a tough job for Olive to tackle particularly the boys of fourteen and fifteen, and that, too, without the use of force: "On her school there were pupils older and bigger than she was. It required great tact to be a school teacher. To keep order among the big undisciplined boys without pistol and bull whip was a difficult and dangerous business." Teaching is another name for duties and obligations. Besides her teaching work, Olive is supposed to work on other fronts as well. She is a master to the school and is supposed to handle every situation on her own. To her pupils in the class, she is a teacher; to the sick and the unwell, she is expected to become a nursing mother: "Olive had also to practise a rudimentary medicine, for there were constant accidents. She sewed-up knife cuts after a fight in the school-yard. When a small barefooted boy was bitten by a rattle snake, it was her duty to suck his toe to draw the poison out." She is to her pupils in school what a mother is to her children at home. As a mother looks after the comfort of the family members, a teacher in school goes into the minute details of her pupils. She is there to make her pupils culturally and educationally sound.

A teacher in Steinbeck is not only a custodian of her pupils' moral, educational, and spiritual growth, she is also responsible for the development of the community and society she is living in. Olive fits herself perfectly into the prescribed role: "In addition, the whole social life of the area was in her hands, not only graduation exercises, but dances, meetings, debates, Chorals, Christmas and May Day festivals, patriotic exudations on Decoration Day and the Fourth of July. She was on the election board and headed and held together all charities." Olive skillfully manages her job in school and with an equal skill she discharges her duties towards society. She possesses the managerial efficiency of her mother, Liza Hamilton. Olive, too, like Elizabeth, leaves her job after marriage and becomes the mistress of her home, discharging her household obligations with an equal efficiency.

Steinbeck's teachers are self-reliant, courageous women. Most of the teachers in Steinbeck come of rural backgrounds where job is almost a necessity. Whereas for Elizabeth and Olive it is a mental necessity, for Miss Martin and Miss Morgan it is a financial necessity, too. They have the security of their homes to give financial support tothe other members of the family. Their education and their profession have given them tremendous courage to face their destinies both at home and at schools. Their education and profession have helped them gain confidence and self-assuredness. They are better placed than the domestic women of Steinbeck but they do not fall into the category of radical feminists. In their relationship to men they are as traditional as the domestic daughters of Steinbeck are.

II

Businesswomen

Another category of professional women, which comes next to the category of teachers, is that of businesswomen. Out of the three businesswomen in the three different novels, two are running their own restaurants and one is running a boutique for ladies, specializing in fashionable dresses of the time. Alice Chicoy in *The Wayward Bus* is a lone example in the whole professional world of Steinbeck who is married and is continuing with her profession of running a restaurant, too. As a result, she remains an incomplete Women—a Women who badly fails to meet the demands of her professional and domestic roles. Her failure at both the fronts leads to her frustration finding expression in frequent bouts of anger and irritation. She is a tough worker who is independently running a restaurant, thus, helping her husband in the hard times of inflation. She is running the restaurant well, keeping it neat and clean, free from dust and disease. However, in spite of her efficient handling of her business matters, she spoils the whole atmosphere with her arrogance. She is devoid of love and affection, which Steinbeck's domestic figures possess. She treats her subordinates, Norma and Pimples, cruelly. She can easily hurt the feelings of others. She is a bad-tempered Women and never hesitates to insult others. Her violent fits of anger make Norma leave her job and move on with Camille Oaks to find another job for herself.

Alice is just the opposite of Ma Joad. Ma Joad can sacrifice even her share of food if only she can bring contentment to others; whereas Alice cannot spare a bedroom for a night for the stranded bus passengers. She keeps on grumbling and complaining till her bedroom has been vacated by the Pritchards. Mr. Pritchard, who himself feels guilty of occupying her bedroom and bathroom causing her inconvenience, pleads that they must be served breakfast in the room as Mrs. Pritchrd is unwell. What he receives in return is the anger of Alice: "Alice lowered her head like an angry milk-cow. 'Look, I want to go to the toilet and wash my face and you're holding up my bedroom.' " She does not take a minute in insulting her guests, even putting them to grave embarassment. She efficiently manages the restaurant work, keeping things in order, but she is a bad businessWomen who does not know how to deal with her customers.

Alice's bad temperament not only spoils her chances of

running a good business but also removes her husband far away from her. She is a Women of weak mind. She loves Juan but lacks the faith that Steinbeck's other women have in their husands. She is all the time suspicious of Juan's behaviour, and it is only due to her nagging attitude that Juan gets sexually involved with Mildred Pritchard. Alice fails on both the fronts; she fails to satisfy her customers as also her husband. In a subtle way, the two failures are related to each other. Besides, her failure is representative of the period; it has something to do with the times.

Another businessWomen, who is running an independent restaurant like Alice Chicoy, is Ella in *Sweet Thursday*. As a contrast to Alice Chicoy, Ella is unmarried whose entire centre of attention is her restaurant. She excels in her business. As the town does not provide a booming business for her, she herself manages the administrative and the service parts; she herself is the owner and the waitress. She is a Women of tough muscles. From morning till evening she is busy in her restaurant. As there is no helper, she is never off shift.

Ella is a caring mother to her customers. She takes deep interest in the personal lives of her visitors. She enquires after the health of Joe Blaikey's wife and suggests that he should give her tonics and let her have complete rest. She shows concern for the new entrant Suzy. She serves her with a fresh cup of coffee. She is also bothered about her boarding and lodging and even offers Suzy her services in the matter. She tells Suzy that if she needs a room to live in she can talk to her sister who rents out rooms. She makes her customers feel comfortable with her pleasing personality. She lets Suzy leave her suitcase in her restaurant until she gets some suitable place to settle in.

Ella possesses the compassion of Ma Joad. Although she

cannot afford it from the viewpoint of business, she admits Suzy in her restaurant on compassionate grounds. Suzy is out of job after leaving the brothel house of Fauna. She comes to Ella and pleads with her to give her the job of a waitress and shows her readiness to do the job just for two square meals a day. Although Ella finds it economically impossible to accommodate her, still she gives Suzy the shelter the latter requires at the moment. Giving her tired smile she asks Suzy to go and take over the charge of the restaurant.

Another professional, Dessie Hamilton in *East of Eden*, is shown in the business of dress designing. She is the most gay person among the women of Steinbeck. She spreads laughter and gaiety all around. Sometimes women and children visit Dessie simply to keep themselves fit for the day. Dessie carries excitement in her arms as her father Samuel had. For instance, Mrs. Morrison, who visits Dessie to colour her day, is all smiles when she returns: "When she came our eyes would be wet with tears and her nose red and streaming. Walking home, she would dab her nose and wipe her eyes and laugh all over again." Dessie's infectious of laughter adds new charm to her business. Women coming to her are doubly benefitted; they get a good, fashionable dress along with a heartful laughter. Dessie's sincerity towards her business makes it flourishing. However, despite her success, her priority remains marriage. She falls in love with a man but loses the game. She could easily get another man but she would rather stay sincere to the man she loved: "You would have thought that in time she would have got over her first love affair and found another love, but she did not come to think of it, none of the Hamiltons, with all their versatility, had any versatility in love. None of them seemed capable of light or changeable love." Dessie's failure in love shatters her completely and she loses interest in business. Resultantly, her business begins to fall off. She keeps on doing whatever is required of her from the viewpoint of business but without the glow. Dessie's friends share her happiness, but they do not want to be sad with her: "Dessie's friends were good and loyal but they were human, and humans love to feel good and they hate to feel bad.... They weren't disloyal. They didn't want to be sad as much as they wanted to be happy." Women visiting Dessie's shop never realize that what they want from Dessie is happiness and not just the dresses.

Steinbeck's women also possess untiring patience for undergoing hardships. Dessie faces the failure of her lost love affair herself and never lets others have any idea of her mental agony. No one ever comes to know the reason of a sudden change over her. Samuel Hamilton's death is almost the final blow to the already broken Dessic. After her father's death she decides to sell off her business and go back to the ranch to live with Tom. All of Hamilton daughters are strong willed persons. Will, the elder brother of Dessie, tries to persuade her not to go to the ranch, but Dessie's decision is final.

Despite her disturbed mental state, Dessie gives company to her lonely brother, Tom. She does not let Tom know a bit of her mind. She had lots of friends in the valley but no confidants: "Only when Dessie went to her bed did her loss fall on her, bleak and unendurable." She looks after Tom and tries to make life more comfortable and liveable for him. Her agony remains a secret with her. She lives with it and dies with it. She never bothers Tom even about her physical suffering. Only when she comes to realize that her end has come she calls Tom for help: "Dessie lay in her bedroom and her will battled the pain. About ten O'clock in the evening her will began to lose its flight. She called 'Tom! Tom!' " Dessie lives for others but suffers alone; despite her suffering, she provides others with laughter and comfort.

Steinbeck's professional women are successful because of their single-mindedness. They are not the women of divided interests. If they are domestic women, they are all for their homes, and if they are professionals they are all for their professions. In Steinbeck, a Women of divided interests can never be successful. For instance, Alice Chicoy is married Women and again a businessWomen simultaneously. Result is her failure at both the fronts.

III

Artists

Another category of professional women in Steinbeck consists of young artists. Though only two full-fledged artist figures appear in his novels, there is a large number of others who wish to be regular artists, but never quite succeed in their ambitions. For instance, there is Curley's wife in *Of Mice and Men* who wanted to be a movie star. Mordeen of *Burning Bright* is in her parental profession of circus. Clotilde in *The Short Reign of Pippin IV* at one time had worked in the films. But all of them choose to be housewives first. Marriage remains their first preference, profession only secondary. Even Suzanne and Camille Oaks, the two full-fledged artist figures, would have preferred to be housewives if the circumstances had permitted them.

Camille Oaks in a *The Wayward Bus* plays at "stags". She is forced to enter the profession because she fails to keep an ordinary job. She is good at typing but cannot continue with her clerical job because "offices went to pieces when she was hired." Camille is *bold* and brave. She takes the bold decision of joining the stags. She knows well that her profession will never allow her to fulfill her dream of marriage; still she risks her chance of marriage thinking it better to take off clothes at stags and make fifty dollars than "having them torn off in an office." She is a rebel in the real sense. Revolting against the nasty ways of men who all want the same thing from her, she runs a racket and earns well. Instead of surrendering herself to the lust of men, she sacrifices her natural desire for a nice house in a nice town with a man of her own choice and two children. She is a practical Women, a realist who knows that this is the only thing in her profession which she is not going to ever get; given a chance, Camille still would prefer to settle down in a married life.

Camille is sharp enough to recognize the simplicity and sincerity of Norma. She feels safe in her company and makes friends with her. She becomes a comforting mother to the docile Norma and helps her in gaining confidence in life. Like an angel guardian she transforms her into a new Norma. Camille changes her whole appearance so much that even "Norma took a long astonished look at herself." Camille possesses the compassion of all Steinbeckian women. She consoles Norma who is scared of life in a big town. She assures her of a good job and a comfortable stay in the unknown city. She, in fact, acts as a godmother to Norma and tries to relieve her of her troubled mind and help her become her natural self.

Suzanne Lescault, another artist figure in Steinbeck's *The Short Reign of Pippin IV*, is a gifted artist. As a young, school child, she is greatly liked by one and all for her talent for dance and acting: "Suzanne Lescault was a pretty child, with a thin, true singing voice and a natural ability as a dancer so that she dominated the pageants and little plays of the school. Inevitably Suzanne rose from wood sprite to fairy queen to Pierrette, and later, for three successive years, she acted *Joan the Maid* to the complete satisfaction of its authoress, the Sister Superior." Though endowed with such a rich talent for dance, music and acting, Suzanne, never wanted to use her talent for earning money. She wants to pursue it as a hobby only. Like Camille Oaks and all other young girls of Steinbeck, she wants to marry and lead a comfortable life: "In the normal course of events Suzanne would have married and retired her talents and her blossoming figure." But she falls a victim to circumstances. Her father commits suicide, leaving the bruden of a sick mother and a dwarf school-going brother on the young shoulders of Suzanne. Suzanne faces the hard blows of fate bravely. She does not lose heart. Uncomplainigly, she makes her way in the world. She is one of those selfless women of Steinbeck who sacrifice their own desires for the welfare of others. Here, for the sake of her sick mother, and her school-going brother, Suzanne is forced to make her talent her profession.

Suzanne is a Women of high integrity. She shows great sincerity towards her sick mother and younger brother. She is equally dutiful and sincere in her profession. She earns a name for her employers with her natural talens: "Suzanne was employed by the Folies Bergere, where her voice, her grace, and her high and perfect bosom were instantly appreciated and utilized." Almost for twenty years Suzanne serves her employers and graces the stage of the Folies with speaking, singing, and dancing. Suzanne depends on her brother and waits for the time he can take over the burden from her shoulders. But destiny has a different design for her. Her brother's untimely death in an accident makes it almost impossible for her to leave her well-paid position; smilingly She continues with her job and takes care of her 'professionally' ill mother. It is only after the death of her mother that she is able to leave the job and join the convent.

Suzanne the artist becomes Sister Haycinthe. She is as proficient in her new role as she was in the role of an artist. As an artist, she had earned a name for herself and for her employers: "and as a nun Sister Haycinthe radiated such peace and piety that she became an ornament to her order, while her knowledge and background made her both tolerant and helpful to younger sisters with troubles." She acts as an advisor to her childhood friend, Marie Pippin, who comes to seek Suzanne's counsel on difficult matters. She becomes an informal advisor to Marie's husband, Pippin, when he becomes the king of France. She is wise and intelligent and, like all other ideal figures of Steinbeck, possesses a thorough knowledge of men, though she herself is unmarried. While talking to Marie Pippin she says of men: " '...men are either children or old—there is nothing in between." Suzanne possesses unending patience for bearing tragedy. In spite of the great disasters she is confronted with, she remains intact and does not lose interest in life. Both these artist figures of Steinbeck come of a background where job is a financial necessity. Both of them work either to support themselves or to give financial aid to their family members. They are bold and courageous and have the guts to face their destinies.

IV

Waitresses

Next and the last class of women among the professionals is that of waitresses and housemaids. Like teachers, waitresses start appearing in Steinbeck's fiction of the 30s. In *The Grapes of Wrath*, there is reference to a waitress working in a roadside restaurant. Besides Norma, Annie and Suzy, who are depicted at length, there are a number of other waitresses who just receive passing references. Annie in *The Moon Is Down* is a housemaid turned patriot by a sudden twist of incidents. Annie's country has been captured and the Mayor, in whose house she is working, has been kept under house arrest. Irritated by the presence of so many unknown persons around her, Annie throws boiling water on some soldiers. The incident is given a patriotic colour. It is thought that she is annoyed at being made a slave. Annie, the dependable expert cook, overnight becomes Annie, the dependable patriot: "Indeed what for years had been cosidered simply a bad disposition, was suddenly become a patriotic emotion. Annie had gained some little reputation as an exponent of liberty by throwing hot water on the soldiers. She would have thrown it on anyone who cluttered up her porch, but it just happened that she had become a heroine; and since anger had been the beginning of her success, Annie went on to new successes by whipping herself into increased and constant anger."(p.73) Annie is bold and courageous. She hates to be stared at. When she suspects foul intentions on the part of the soldiers, she punishes them by throwing boiling water on them and by even biting one of them. She is a self-respecting Women. She sells off her services for money, but not her self-respect. Annie is a free Women living in a free country.

Annie is sharp and intelligent in contrast to Mrs. Mayor. She is only a servant, but she can assess any situation far better than the mistress of the house. For instance, she knows well, and declares also, that if Alex is tried, people will become rebellious and vocal; they will come out in the streets to avenge the trial of innocent Alex. Servants like Annie and Joseph can foresee what is going to happen in future, whereas women like Mrs. Mayor remain unaware of it. After that incident of the soldiers, Annie gets actively involved in the freedom-struggle of her country. She becomes a faithful soldier of the Mayor and acts as a spy for him. The Mayor appreciates Annie for her efficiency and skill: " 'I don't know what i'd do without her,' he said. 'She gets everywhere, she sees and hears everything.' " Annie holds an important position in the inner circle of the Mayor. She is so much trusted by the Mayor that he assigns her the duty of looking after the Madame in his absence: "And Orden said, 'Annie, I want you to stay with Madame as long as she needs you. Don't leave her alone.' " With her proficient ways of doing things Annie gains a position for herself in society.

Another Women in the same class is Norma in *The Wayward Bus*, who works as a waitress at Alice Chicoy's restaurant. Her profession is only a stop-gap arrangement for her. Her real goal in life is to get married and settle down in a family life. Norma is an inexperienced, impractical and a romantic young girl, who is intensely in love with the imaginary picture of a Hollywood actor, Clark Gable. She writes love-letters to her imaginary lover. She is a grown-up Women with the mind of a child. She has no real exposure to the outside world. Her only contact is with the people coming to the restaurant for a cup of tea, coffee, or for little refreshment. This momentary contact is not sufficient to give her understanding of men and matters. In fact, she has very little knowledge about life. Camille Oak's sympathetic attitude towards Norma makes her bold and decisive. For instance, she decides to leave Alice's job within minutes and moves to Hollywood in search of better opportunities for herself. This shows that she has the potential to go ahead in life, but she never gets any chance to exploit that potential.

Steinbeck's women never get desperate even in the face of worst crisis. They never lose interest in life. Suzy is one such a Women of Steinbeck in *Sweet Thursday* who comes of a broken home. She is cheated in marriage, loses her child, becomes a typist, joins the brothel house of Fauna, and works finally as a waitress only to become the wife of Doc. Marriage remains Suzy's foremost interest; profession to her is only a means to survival. If there were a man to depend upon, to provide her with food and shelter, to give her the comforts of home and children, Suzy would not have bothered about a profession. She is a misfit in the brothel house of Fauna; in fact, she enters the profession only to find some foothold for herself. Similarly, her job as a waitress is a temporary arrangement only. Her goal is marriage with a man like Doc, and as soon as she gets the chance to realize her dreams she grabs it. Suzy, the hustler, the skillful waitress, thus, goes to become a skillful house manager.

Thus, the women of profession in Steinbeck are vitally different from the domestic women,who remain a dominant type in the writer's canon. These professional women are reflections of the "new Women" of the modern era between the two World Wars. Showing greater self-reliance and confidence these women make attempts to assume the new role of out-of-home life in America. Competing with men in the commercial world of individual struggle, they throw away the bonds of domesticity and strive for independence from and equality with men. Of course, the professional women in Steinbeck are not as radical and daring as they are in Hemingway and Fitzgerald, but they do make a great departure from the traditional mode of life represented by the domestic women in his novels. Even these women of profession in Steinbeck share with the domestic women their overriding instinct for love and marriage. In more favourable circumstances, they will sacrifice their professions for love and marriage. Also, in Steinbeck's fiction these "new" women do not constitute, as they do in Faulkner, and even in Hemingway, the negative poles or disruptive forces in the writer's projected order of life. Standing half-way between feminist radicalism and tame domesticity they represent a middle position between the two—a position which excludes the excesses of the two and includes and combines the better qualities of both. Avoiding the aggressiveness of radical feminism and the submissiveness of conservative domesticity they uphold the more balanced values of self-respect and self-reliance. It is because of their adoption of the less angular middle path that they remain more attractive even while practising, at times, the demeaning professions like that of the prostitute.

Notes

1. R.S. Hughes, *Beyond 'The Red Pony'* (1987) 43.
2. *East of Eden*, 142.
3. *Ibid.*, 46.
4. *Ibid.*, 141.
5. *To a God Unknown*, 45.
6. *Ibid.*

Conclusion

From its very origin the American society clung to the sexual division of labour which assigned women primarily the responsibility for the proper maintenance of the family and men the responsibility for its economic support. The traditional cult of domesticity prevailed even in the 20th century America and women were still viewed basically as mothers and wives first. Home was the Women's sphere to which Man retreated for physical and spiritual refreshment. Here, he found shelter from the anxieties of modern world. It was a sanctuary for moral and spiritual values that could not survive in the outside world without the domestic support. And at the centre of the home was a Women—the custodian of man's moral and spiritual growth. But strangely enough even when Women was cast in this all important role of a spiritual saviour of the nation, the strong bias against her mental capabilities continued in one way or the other. Economically dependent on men, women were viewed as intellectually inferior to men and, thus, were kept in a subordinate position. They were thought to be incapable of making decisions, unfit for any vocation that demanded sharp intellectual acumen and, thus, they were invariably kept out of the professional world. If at all they were allowed any work outside home, it was only as nurses, housemaids and labourers or at best as teachers—all soft professions best suited to the compassionate nature of women.

The Feminist movement, started in the mid 19th century, failed to bring any significant change in the status of ordinary American women till 1960 when the movement regained its lost momentum. It definitely won women the right to vote in the 1920s through the Nineteenth Amendment but it completely failed to root out the social prejudices against women. It also failed to change the mental make up of women themselves who opposed the very idea of women moving out of their homes. The suffragists had hoped that after the right to vote women would act as a cohesive force to bring about social and political changes. They had hoped that "pure in spirit, selfless in motivation, and dedicated to the preservation of human life, female voters would remake society and turn government away from war and corruption."[1] But the poor response of the women voters came as a blow to the suffragist movement and hopes of its protagonists. Elections of the 1920s showed a low turn out of women voters. It was really difficult to remove the deep-rooted cultural belief of women that their place was in the home and politics was a male domain only. Majority of women showed utter indifference to politics. Most women who failed to vote, when interviewed at that time, responded that they failed to vote because their husbands failed to remind them of it. And the ones who exercised their right to vote, voted like their husbands. There were also those who commented that females should stay at home and leave politics to men. Thus, the condition of women, for practical purposes, did not improve much even after they got the right to vote as the feminists had hoped that it would.

From the feminist point of view, we may even say that the condition of women rather took a turn for the worse in the 20s. The career-conscious women of the early twentieth century were now replaced by the job-seeking women. Career was only secondary to the latter class; it is better to say that it was a stop-gap arrangement before marriage. Young college women preferred to work only till they got married and began to raise families. Very few girls entering adulthood in the 20s "had the crusading spirit and desire for professional success that had characterized so many of their predecesors in the previous generation. This change was particularly marked among college graduates, an increasing number of whom expressed a preference for marriage over any other life-style."[2] Despite their desire for work, their first priority remained the traditional one—that is, marriage, shelter of a home, dependence on a man of their own and children. Thus, generally women did not relish the idea of working outside homes after they got married; but if at all they wished to be in jobs after marriage, they could not do so for there was particular antagonism to working wives. In the first place, employers almost everywhere in the country refused to employ married women. Secondly, women were bombarded with messages from magazines, movies and colleges to value marriage and children above all else. Repeatedly they were told that the domestic shpere should be the most satisfying one for women. This kind of pressure from society to keep women at home and out of competition in the professional world remained very strong till very recently, say till the end of the 60s. So, most women in jobs during the decade invariably were unmarried and they, too, remained in job only till they got married.

This status of women as discussed and delineated in the 20s spilled over to the early 30s, too. An overwhelming majority of women continued to see marriage as the main goal of their lives and young girls, both rural and urban, came to work only till they were finally settled in matrimony. In Steinbeck's novel *To a God Unknown* Elizabeth McGreggor is a teacher who sticks to her job till she finds her man because at the moment "most women expected to work several years after college, but only until they married and began to raise families."[3] Similarly, young rural women often "left their farms to continue their schooling in town, or more typically to find wage-paying jobs in non-rural areas."[4] Miss Martin and Miss Morgan are two young teachers in Steinbeck's novel *The Pastures of Heaven* who leave their homes to work as paid servants so that they may support their families in rural areas. Paulette in *Cup of Gold* is one other example of a rural Women who comes out of her home to work as a domestic servant to supplement the family income.

However, an unprecedented economic crisis gripped America in the 30s in the form of the Great Depression. The whole socio-economic scenario then underwent a vast change. Whatever little doors of the professional world had opened up to women in the first three decades of the century, were now closed on them with a bang. During the Depression, there was scarcity of jobs and the women who had entered jobs only in the recent past were asked to go back to their old nest—the home. Barbara J. Harris rightly sums up the situation when she writes: "If the 1920s saw a showing down of the entrance of women into the professions, the 1930s spelled disaster. Under the impact of the depression, hostility to female employment reached new levels of intensity. There was virtually unanimous opinion that women should not compete for the scarce jobs with men who had families to support. Implicit in the this view was the assumption that females did not have families to support and therefore had less right to employment than men."[5] In the 30s stress was, thus, mainly on women going back to their homes, limiting their aspirations to husband, family and domesticity and assuming their primary responsibility for all household chores.

For more than one reason, during the decade, this prejudice against women working for a profession was very strong in the case of married women. As Susan Ware testifies: "Working women, especially, if they were married, faced strong public hostility to their very participation in the work force."[6] Many States literally passed legislation restricting the employment of married women. Almost every employer was allergic to hiring wives as employees. The reason generally given for not allowing married women to enter the professional world was that Women's place was in the home and that "children were healthier and home life happier if women did not work."[7] Again, women themselves found it difficult to combine their double whole time jobs of home and office satisfactorily. The traditional bread winners did not object to the additional income coming to their homes but they refused to share the household burden of women. Resultantly, the working women, sharing the double burden of home and office, could not do justice to the two. They had to neglect one for the sake of the other. Their negligence of their jobs naturally made them inferior workers in the eyes of their employers. As home remained the prime responsibility of women, their negligence at the home front could not be tolerated either. A Women who sacrificed her household responsibilities for the sake of her professional aspirations came under severe attack through writings and movies. The Captain's wife in Steinbeck's *Cannery Row* is an apt illustration of the point. She fulfills her political ambitions at the cost of her husband's happiness. She makes her husband's life miserable to achieve her professional success. Steinbeck portrays her in such a way that the reader's sympathies are with the Captain. She has been made to look a villain. Women deviating from their traditional role of providing emotional maintenance to their men in home were never spared by the American society.

America at this juncture seems to have discovered anew the importance of the Women's role in the home, especially at a moment of crisis. She was considered the one who could sustain man amidst the depressing realitis of the outer world. Women were often relied on to carry heavier burdens in moments of such crises than men because "women know that life must go on and that the needs of life must be met and it is their courage and determination which, time and agian, have pulled us through worse crises than the present one."[8] These words of Eleanor Roosevelt immediately remind us of Steinbeck's Ma Joad who shows the same enduring courage in times of deprivation. Ma Joad echoes the words of Mrs. Roosevelt when she talks of Women's strength in hard times: " 'Man, he lives in jerks—baby born an' a man dies, an' that's a jerk—gets a farm an' loses his farm, an' that's a jerk. Women, it's all one flow, like a stream, little eddies, little waterfalls, but the river, it goes right on. Women looks at it like that .' "[9] Ma Joad's courage and patience, warmth and endurance prevent the Joad family from breaking up and in this context her role at the centre of the family assumes great significance. In fact, Eleanor's words remind us of all the indestructible women-figures of Steinbeck who show their real character in difficult times.

Roles of the male and the female thus clearly demarcated, we find that women in the 30s stepped out of their homes only when goaded by economic necessity. If at all they ventured into the professional world, it was not because they sought liberation from the burdens of domesticityor because they enjoyed new equality with men in the job-market but because it was absolutely necessary for them to supplement the meagre economic resources of the family and save it from starvation. Majority of the American women in the late 30s worked as unpaid domestic labourers within their homes; only a minority worked outside the home at paid employment. This perhaps is the reason that in Steinbeck's fiction of the late 30s there are no working women worth the name. The only exception is Curley's wife in *Of Mice and Men* who wanted to be in the show business but could not do so as "the theatre district was hurt by the Depression."[10] In her frustration she married Curley whom she never liked. On the whole, the Depression period, we find, reinforced women's traditional role of mothers and wives. No wonder, the image of Women that emerges in the novels of Steinbeck during the decade is that of a powerful mother-figure or earth-mother as illustrated in the characters of Mother Morgan in *Cup of Gold*, Rama Wayne and Elizabeth Wayne in *To a God Unknown*, Katherine Sharkwicks and Alicia Whiteside in *The Pasturs of Heaven*, Mama Torres in the short story *"Flight,"* Jody's mother in the short novel *"The Red Pony"* and Ma Joad in *The Grapes of Wrath*. All these indestructible mother-figures of Steinbeck provide emotional and spiritual strength to their men as also to all others in the family.

In retrospect, we, thus, see that American women in the late 30s, in spite of being placed on a high pedestal in the field of domesticity, faced many problems in work force. First, they were given limited options in the professional field. They were allowed to become teachers, nurses or housemaids only. Second, for the same job men got higher wages than women. Women were paid less for the same quantity and quality of work for which men got high wages. Third, women were not allowed to take up administrative posts. Though women dominated the field of teaching, there were no women employed as administrators in the field of education. All administrative posts were invariably occupied by men. Perhaps all these prejudices lessened the charm of career for women.

The 1940s, from the Women's point of view, can be divided into three phases. First phase consists of the period from 1940 to 1945, the period of World War II, when public hostility to married women working outside home did soften a bit for a short while because of the manpower crisis during the World War II; but it did not root out completely the objections to women moving outside home. It was the time when mass media joined hands with the government in persuading women to join the work force. The second phase consists of the period from 1945 to 1946 which witnessed a massive lay off of married women from the work force. The mass media which had encouraged women at the beginning of the decade to enter the professional fields now started telling them that their place was in the home and that they should leave their jobs in favour of the returning soldiers. The third phase consists of the period form 1947 to 1950 when married women once again were forced to enter the professional field because of inflation and steep rise in demand of the consumer goods.

Coming to the first phase, we find that though hostility to working wives and mother still prevailed, the overall employment scenario for women changed a lot during the wartime. As the Great Depression swept the country, it had become less and less likely that women would ever enter the male-dominated careers. But the coming of World War II radically transformed the whole scene for women. During the first few months of the defense crisis, the attitudes of the 1930s prevailed. But the Japanese attack on Pearl Harbour in 1941 swiftly eliminated opposition to hiring women workers. With an unprecedented skill women labour force replaced their menfolk who had joined army. Now the mass media joined hands with the government in inspiring women to join the labour force. As states William H. Chafe: "A few years earlier, newspapers and magazines had discouraged women from leaving the home and had supported restrictions on the hiring of married women. Now radio stations and periodicals glamourized war work and pleaded with women to hurry and enlist at their local employemtn office."[11] For the first time in thirty years, Women's economic status changed significantly.

But even in this favourable wartime situation discrimination on the economic front against women in general and married women in particular persisted. They continued to get low wages for the same job for which men had been getting higher. They were still kept out of top policy-making administrative posts. Businesswomen were expected to work as trainees rather than as executives. The wife who worked outside home and also took care of her family carried two full-time jobs on her hands. Her dual responsibility prevented her from functioning at the same level of efficiency as a man in the world of business and labour. Rightly says Ernest R. Groves about the working women during the wartime: "If they are married, there is one difference between them and men. Their occupation is generally less secure. However acceptable they may be to their fellow workers as individuals, they encountered from the unmarried women and from the married men attitudes that express opposition by both these competitors tothe idea of the married women working. They also often felt the strain that comes from being a wife, a mother, and in some degree a housekeeper, in additon to being a wage earner."[12] Perhaps this is the same strain of coping with the two entirely different worlds which results into the bad tantrums of Alice Chicoy in Steinbeck's *The Wayward Bus*. Many women workers who were full-time housewives found it impossible to do both jobs without either succumbing to exhaustion or taking time off from work. Neglecting household chores could never be tolerated on the part of a Women. It was inexcusable as is the case with Captain's wife in Steinbeck's *Cannery Row*. That's why married women still faced the hostility of public as well as employers. They were discouraged from taking up jobs, especially married women with young children.

Whatever the progress, whatever the changes that occurred in the field of women employment during World War II, the question that bothered most Americans, the male and the female, was whether the change would be permanent. Attitude of the government and the employers was a clear indication that the change was only a temporary one. Traditional attitudes towards women had changed only a little. Susan M. Hartmann explains the change in clear terms:

> The public discourse on women's new wartime roles established three conditions which set limits on social change. The first was that women were replacing men in the world outside the home only "for the duration." Particularly, during the later stages of the war, employers and public officials asserted that women workers were proud of their contributions to the war effort, but were eager to return to the home and would gladly relinquish

> their jobs to returning soldiers. The second conditon was that women would retain their "femininity" even as they perfomed masculine duties.... Finally, the media emphasized the eternal feminine motivations behind women's willingness to step out of customary roles.... In the public image, women took war jobs to bring their men home more quickly and to help make the world a more secure place for their children. Thus, as women moved into the public spheres, they were reminded that their new positions were temporary, that retaining the traditional feminine characteristics was essential, and that their familial roles continued to take precedence over all others.[13]

Female relationship to the professional world during this decade thus can well be called a marriage of necessity. Most Americans, female as well as male, still believed that the primary responsibility of wives and mothers was to care for the household and to rear children. Despite the greater number of women entering into jobs, the social outlook for women remained unchanged. Home, husband and children remained Women's primary duty—a duty which she could not lay aside, no matter what the circumstances were.

With the peacetime back in force, the same media which had encouraged women to join the labour force in the wartime, now started dissuading them from sticking to their jobs. They were encouraged and reinforced by a powerful media appeal to return to their homes, thus, leaving jobs for the traditional breadwinners. The retreat to the home of millions of women was based in part on a personal decision. As states William H. Chafe: "A substantial number of Americans, however, believed that the time had come for women to return to the home. Many observers viewed women's work as a primary cause of Juvenile delinquency and believed that the continued presence of wives and mothers in the labour force directly threatened the stability of the nation's social institutions."[14] The period between 1945 to 1946 witnessed a massive layoff of women labour force. Pre-war norms were reiterated and it was untiringly repeated that women owed their full-time attention to the home and family only. Most of them who left their jobs went back to unpaid work as housewives and mothers. Everyone was so glad to get back to normal living after the war that great emphasis was laid on family-life and Women's place in the home.

There is another shift in the scene in the late 40s when rising prices forced women, especially the middle class women to reenter the professional world. One income was not sufficient to fulfill the basic needs of a family. During the early 40s Women's work was a national necessity and in the last part of the decade inflation and rising consumer demands legitimized Women's work. Though once again more and more women entered the labour force in the late 40s, there was a good majority of them still who refused to retain their former positions even if the job was available. Theirs was a voluntary withdrawal from the labour force, perhaps because they found it difficult to bear the strains of combining housekeeping with paid employment. The women who retained their jobs had to face a complicated set of options. They worked from nine to five and still were expected to be full-time homemakers. They faced the difficulty of resolving the conflicting priorities in their lives. They remained in a dilemma and did not know what to choose and how to choose. Public opinion was still against married women moving outside their homes. Though women's job was a necessity at the moment, still only those married women were allowed in the labour force whose children were grown up and no longer required the supervision of their mothers.

Voluntary withdrawal of women from the labour force in the late 40s gave birth to a conspicuous increase in the marriage and birth rate. Barbara J. Harris records that from 1945 to 1960 "the average age of marriage for American women dropped to the lowest level anywhere in the Western World. The birth rate soared especially among the college educated. For the first time they had as many children as the poor. Even among the best educated females, marriage took precedence over professions. There was an increasing feeling that families and careers could not be combined, and most women opted for the former. The only feminist ideal of the single, professional women almost completely disappeared."[15] Popular media continued celebrating marriage and motherhood. College women during this period were marrying at younger ages and with greater frequency, and they were bearing more children. They believed that the prime motive of college education should be to prepare girls for marriage and family responsibilities, to make them full-time housemakers. Families in backward areas still continued to support the higher education of sons than that of daughters. If at all women entered the field of higher education, they never attended college "primarily to prepare for a vocation. Anticipation of marriage and maternity dominated their educational motives. Most college women expected to work until marriage or motherhood, and a minority of these hoped to resume employment after they had raised their families."[16] The overall picture of the status of women in the late 1940s, say after 1947, was that more and more women were taking up their traditional roles. More women married than ever before and at younger ages. Birth rate was almost doubled during this period.

Popular films of the time glorified women's domestic roles. In films "career women were implicitly criticized for their coldness and ambition, while their fates suggested the incompatibility of professional success with marriage."[17]

The 1950s can easily be described as a decade when traditional values gained new energy and influence. The home remained the central focus of female life with the household chores expanded. Nationwide women got almost crazy to do everything with their own hands. They took pride in decorating their homes, planting gardens and making their own clothes. The revival of popular concern with the home coincided with a substantial exodus tothe suburbs. The suburban way of life added a new dimension to Women's traditional role. As Barbara J. Harris puts it: "The 1950s also saw a mass exodus to suburbia, where wife's primary role was to make her home an oasis of comfort and serenity for the harried male who returned in the evening from the race for economic success in the city. It all seemed like a strangely modern version of the Victorian ethos."[18] Women of the fifties, thus, discovered a new meaning in their traditional role in the house and family. The demands of childrearing, entertaining their husbands and volunteer activities left little time for boredom and provided ample opportunity for fulfillment. Mary Mchugh briefly but beautifully sums up the situation in the 50s: "If a Women was not happy leading a domestic life, there was something wrong with her."[19]

In the 50s, thus, house remained the central focus of attention for women and household chores were never relegated tothe background. But with the last child sent off to school, women had hardly anything left to occupy their mind and body. With no full-time occupation in hand, women sought a job outside home. They were still expected to work as full-time homemakers. The income they earned contributd to the higher education of their children but men never thought of sharing the household responsibilities with women. Primarily, they still were housewives first and working women next. They were allowed to work only after their children no longer required full-time supervision. This almost is beautifully summed up by Mary Mchugh in the words: "Thou shalt stay home and take care of those children until they are in college or working or else you will have neurotic, miserable children and a husband who leaves you for a Women who loves cleaning the house."[20] Steinbeck lived in an age when Women's traditional role of a mother and a wife was valued and this perhaps is the reason that Women's image that emerges most strongly and impressively in the novels of Steinbeck is the image of powerful mother figure.

The professional status of young unmarried women in the 50s underwent a change. Whereas during the period befoe 1945 women were generally allowed to become teachers, nurses and housemaids only, after their reentry in the professional world in the late 50s, they were given a wider choice. Now young women were entering the fields of independent business. More and more women were entering the field of skilled jobs. That is why whereas in Steinbeck's fiction of the 30s and 40s, his women figures are mainly labourers, teachers and housemaids, in his fiction of the late 40s and 50s, we find them in the role of stage artists and businesswomen, too. In *The Wayward Bus*, written in 1947, we meet Camille Oaks, a young stage artist and Alice Chicoy who is running a roadside restaurant on her own. In the same novel there is another character Norma who leaves her job as a servant in the restaurant to get a better job in the city. In *East of Eden*, there is Dessie Hamilton who is a successful businessWomen, a successful dress-designer along with Olive

Hamilton who is in the profession of teaching. In *Sweet Thursday*, we find Ella who runs a restaurant and Suzy who first becomes a prostitute and then a helpmate to Ella in her restaurant with the intention of getting a good match. In his novel *The Short Regin of Pippin IV*, Suzanne is a stage artist and Clotilde is an artist, a writer, a politician—all at one time or the other—all rolled into one. She never takes her occupation seriously. The only occupation she is interested in is the occupation of motherhood and wifehood. All Steinbeck's working women intend to stick to their profession only till they get married. They all are true representatives of their times where priority with women remained marriage, children and dependence on a man of their own.

Besides the unpaid occupations of motherhood and wifehood and the paid professions of teachers, housemaids, businesswomen and stage artists, one more occupation that Steinbeck's women take up in abundance is the occupation of whoredom as the business of prostitution was a necessary part of the ecosystem of Cannary Row, Monterey and the Salinas Valley—the canvas of all his writings. Whoredom, in his world, however, is a genial profession which is meant to provide companionship and conversation to the lonely farm labourers and the oppressed husbands. The madams in Steinbeck's ficion are matriarchal figures who are primarily carrying out the role of mothers for their girls and clients as well. Whorehouses in Steinbeck are the "sporting houses"—the homes away from homes. The madams here are responsible for the feeding, clothing , health and welfare and sometimes even the future happiness of their girls—in fact, they do everything which a conscientious mother would do for her biological children. They are the very embodiment of motherliness. They not only look after the physical welfare of their girls but also assume responsibility for their moral and spiritual development. They train their girls for the sevice of suffering humanity. For instance, Dora's girls in *Cannery Row*, besides their daily work in the house, go to attend to the sick persons in the town who are down with an epidemic. Madams are, in fact, the custodians of the moral and spiritual development of their girls. They are as worried as a mother in a regular home would be to settle down their girls in their natural roles of wives and mothers. The best example of the type is Fauna in Sweet Thursday who is a successful match-maker for her girls.

Steinbeck does not care to analyse the motives that drive women to prostitution but his portrayal of the Lopez Sisters in *The Pastures of Heaven*, the promiscuous housewives of *Tortilla Flat*, and Suzy in *Sweet Thursday* clearly indicates that one of the factors, and perhaps the major one, responsible for turning these women to prostitution is economic pressure. While portraying these women Steinbeck seems to be agreeing with G.B. Shaw who in "Preface" to *Mrs. Warren's Profession* writes: "Prostitution is caused, not by female depravity and male licentiousness, but simply by underpaying, undervaluing, and overworking women so shamefully that the poorest of them are forced to resort to prostitution to keep body and soul together."[21] The Lopez Sisters in *The Pastures of Heaven* try to make a living through running a Mexican Restaurant. Though they make the finest enchiladas in the valley, business is poor. One day Rose gives herself to a customer, not for money but in gratitude for his eating three enchiladas. From then onwards, the sisters encourage their customers and the business picks up. But the two sisters are put out of business by a jealous wife and they are forced to enter a brothelhouse in San Francisco. They become bad women to support themselves. The promiscuous housewives of *Tortilla Flat* are promiscuous because they have no other source of getting their basic needs like food, cloth and shelter fulfilled. Suzy in *Sweet Thursday* becomes a prostitute only because she has nothing else to support herself. She finds the profession better than waiting on tables or clerking at 'Five and Ten.' Suzy's basic desire is to get married and settle down in a home of her own failing which she becomes a prostitute only temporarily. Steinbeck's whores see no sin in their activities; rather, they are proud of their profession and find prostitution to be a public benefaction. The best exponent of this is Coeur de Gris's mother in *Cup of Gold* who is a "free Women" and proud of her position. In Steinbeck prostitution is a profession like any other profession. In his ficion, the profession is a means to survival. a natural and harmless partime even, and does not carry any stigma with it.

Steinbeck uses prostitution to expose the hypocrisy of conventional morality and to startle the bourgeois by inverting respectable values. He enjoys inverting the traditional morality of sobriety, chastity, etc., in such a way that they are made to look foolish. Robert E. Morsberger observes: "he could use prostitution as a focus for satire, both against puritan prudery and the work ethic and against the hypocrisy of sanctimonious politicians and businessmen who are just as eager customers as the proletariat they put down for immoral habit."[22] He portrays his whores as saints and angels. For instance, the whole incident of the Lopez Sisters is presented in such a manner that they are made to look innocent whereas the society is painted as the real villain, responsible for making them the "bad" women they are. Similarly, the role of Camille Oaks in *The Wayward Bus* of taking off clothes at stags is again decided by the society she lives in. In normal course, the girl would have settled down in a married life but the society chooses the role of a tramp for her. It is not the girl but the society which is to be blamed for what she is. Dora Flood in *Cannery Row* is a philanthropist on whose donations even great religious institutions like the Church thrive. Irony of the situation is that whoredom is illegal but it is all legal to accept the money of shame to run the institutions which discard the profession itself. Steinbeck also suggests that the customers of these houses are very often the so-called pillars of the community such as the city officials or the businessmen. Through prostitution he, thus, intends to attack the hypocrisy of social convention and self-righteousness but instead of resorting to bristling attacks, he contents himself with merely poking mild fun at the double standards maintained by the so-called respectable citizens of society.

Besides historical and sociological factors, Steinbeck's approach to his women characters was strongly influenced by the eminent psychologists of the age who emphasized that the normal life for a Women is one of marriage and children. Steinbeck seems to have been impressed by Freudian psychology of sex and his findings about sexuality. Freud established that anatomy is destiny and for women that meant a destiny circumscribed by their reproductive organs. A happy Women, one who was well-adjusted according to the precepts of Freudian psychology, was one who had fulfilled her role as the bearer of children, adjunct and helpmate and accepted her domination by the male. Psychologists like Freud defined motherhood as the ultimate fulfillment of Women's sexuality. And the women who failed to become mothers were seen as neurotics. In Steinbeck's fiction bearing of children becomes almost a sacred activity. Here all childless women are shown as behaving awakwardly.

They are portrayed as neurotic, selfish and sex-starved characters. Elisa Allen in *"The chrysanthemums,"* Mary Teller in *"The White Quail,"* the anonymous Women in *"The Snake,"* Emma Randall in *"The Harness,"* Mike's wife in *"The Vigilante,"* Captain's wife and Mrs. Malloy in *Cannery Row* and Alice Chicoy in *The Wayward Bus* bear out the truth of Freudian conclusions. All these childless women of Steinbeck show this or that abnormality in their character. Only his sacrificing, selfless mothers or wives are among the happy women—inspired and inspiring in every way.

The most powerful women figures in Steinbeck undisputedly are the maternal figures. These maternal figures, however, owe their existence to a variety of factors. One is certainly the sociological factor already discussed in the previous pages. Steinbeck lived in a time when Women's place in the home was valued. She was considered the soul of the family. There was definitely pressure from society to glorify Women's place in the home. The second factor responsible for portraying and also glorifying motherhood in his fiction is the influence of the thinkers of the time. Thinkers like Freud stated that biologically a natural course of life for a Women is to get married and fulfill her role as the bearer of children. And women deviating from their natural function of mothers become neurotic. Mimi Reisel Gladstein, however, traces the abundance of matriarchal figures in the fiction of Steinbeck to an autobiographical note. He establishes that the existence of powerful mother figures in the fiction of Faulkner, Hemingway and Steinbeck results from the strong influence of their own mothers in the formative years of their childhood. They lived in female-dominated homes and it made all the difference to them though they responded quite differently to their upbringing.

Faulkner remained an admirer of his mother and lived close to his home and visited his mother almost daily. Hemingway, on the contrary, hated his mother to the extent that he did not attend her funeral even. He never visited her and did not allow her to visit him. Steinbeck's response to his strong, influential mother, Olive Steinbeck, was balanced. Though not an admirer of his mother like Faulkner, he went to attend on his mother in her last days of fatal illness. He looked after his mother tenderly and there is no denying the fact that she lived, howsoever indirectly, in almost all his important writings.

Besides this influence of dominant mother figures in the formative years of their lives, both Hemingway and Steinbeck experienced another important female influence in the form of their wives which definitely contributed to the shaping of their literary female figures. The two showed great financial and emotional dependence on their wives all through their lives. Hemingway's writings were financially supported by his first two wives, Hadley and Pauline. His third wife Martha had to pay her own way to marriage. Hemingway's emotional dependence on women is clear from the fact that he married four times and he never left one Women unless he had another one ready to marry him. All his wives were devoted to him completely, always ready to cater to his whims. Likewise, Steinbeck started his married life financially dependent on Carol, who had to work very often to support them both. She used to work at a job all day long and type John's manuscripts at night. Steinbeck's emotional dependence on his first wife Carol was the dependence of a child on his mother. His second and third wife failed to mother him causing him his frequent fits of depression. Critics feel that Steinbeck's best writings came out of those years when he had Carol with him to depend upon, to provide him emotional sustenance. Hemingway and Steinbeck always needed a Women to depend upon—a Women who would mother them, fill them with emotional and spiritual strength.

Steinbeck is generally criticized for not giving any place to romantic love in his fictional world or again for not portraying the new Women in his writings. One may not downright reject the charges and may even concede that these are rather weak areas in our author, but certainly any deficiency on these fronts is to be traced to Steinbeck's approach to life and literature and not to any lack of will or skill on his part.

In the 30s Steinbeck was mainly dealing with the people in whose life there was no place for romantic love. The rural people of California, particularly the people around Salinas Valley, were so engrossed in getting their basic needs for bread, clothes and shelter fulfilled that they had no time or energy left for love. Susan Ware quotes this significant remark of a migrant Women: "love does not exist among the lower classes."[23] Susan Ware also writes that "the women were so tired by all their making do that they were too tired for making love."[24] When sex within marriage had decreased to this extent, sex outside marriage could not be expected. Naturally Steinbeck's fiction of the 30s is definitely devoid of romantic love and there are no references to pre-marital or extra-marital relationship here.

But the picture is different in Steinbeck's fiction of the late 40s and 50s when the scene of his novels shifts from California to New York. Here appear young women like Mildred Pritchard, Camille Oaks, Abra Bacon and Clotilde who are not scared of having romantic love or pre-marital sexual relationship. Mildred Pritchard in *The Wayward Bus* provokes Juan Chicoy to get involved with her in a sexual relationship. Abra Bacon's romantic love in *East of Eden* first with Aron and then with Cal is again representative of the romantic trends prevalent in the American society of the 50s. The story of Clotilde's romantic involvement with Ted Johnson sufficiently shows that Steinbeck's novels are the social documents of his times.

As about the other allegation that Steinbeck does not take up the new Women for his theme in his writings, a critical analysis at our end reveals that Steinbeck attempts to portray in his short stories if not the new Women, at least the free-spirited Women of the 20th century. For instance, Steinbeck's portrayal of Elisa Allen in *"The Chrysanthemums"* illustrates his ability to understand the problems of a Women of energy and ability, a Women isolated from other women and told by her society that her desire for freedom and adventure is not the right kind of thing for a Women. Again, Mary Teller's portrayal in *"The White Quail"* proves that the novelist is able to face the reality of self-sustaining, independent women in non traditional roles.

The socio-cultural background of his times explains this telling absence of new Women in Steinbeck's fiction in general. The Suffragette movement was almost non-existent in America from 1930s to 1960s—the main spell of period over which Steinbeck's writings are spread. The new notions of liberty, equality and breakaway roles had not yet found a popular base in America. The unconventional Womenhood was not yet a solid reality there. As a social realist Steinbeck, therefore, did not find these airy concepts of much real interest to him. Rather, he chose to confine himself to and concentrate on the Women that both traditional and contemporary America presented, cherished and held dear to its heart.

Thus, Steinbeck's writings reflect his social, cultural, historical and somewhat personal limitations where women are concerned, though in matters of sexuality he was a pioneer in overcoming taboos about what it was permissible to portray. For instance, Steinbeck's *The Grapes of Wrath* was banned from high school libraries for its "vulgarity" and it was called "a morbid, filthy-worded novel!" But in his portrayal of Women Steinbeck remains traditional and he assigns his women the traditional female occupations such as mothering, teaching school children and prostitution. All his important women—whether domestic or fallen or working—are possessed with the dominant instinct of motherhood, the basis of the survival of the race. Although his women are traditional mother figures, they are not at all the passive women of Hemingway; on the contrary, they are active and assertive. Even his whores are basically mothers. His working women, too, are preparing themselves for their future role of mothers and wives. The image of Women that, thus, emerges in his fiction—spread over almost half a century—is predominantly that of the creator, the sustainer, the saviour; it is the image of the mother figure symbolizing strength, patience, courage and determination that lends at least part of its greatness and grandeur to the pages that hold it.

A realist portraying the social realities of his times, Steinbeck does not belong to the tradition of the novel represented by Hawthorne, James and Hemingway, who were concerned with the depiction of the American culture in relation to the European and whose major interest is the American identity in the larger context of the Western world. These writers focussed their works on the general aspects of the national character and identity. Steinbeck is also not like Mark Twain or William Faulkner who centred their fictional writings on the questions of regional identities. Compared to these two sets of writers representing the two major streams of the American novel,

Steinbeck is closer to the stream of novel represented by Frank Norris, Theodore Dreiser, Jack London, and William Dean Howells. He shares with these novelists his commitment to realism and naturalism. He focusses his fiction on neither the archetypal Americanism of Hawthorne and James nor on the regional mythicism of Twain and Faulkner but on the specific reality of a period with which he was personally associated. His strength as an artist, of course, lies as much in converting the topical into universal as it does in re-creating the topical. For instance, Steinbeck's novels dealing with the problems of the American peasants and migrants during the period between the two Wars are as timeless in their appeal as they are topical.

Steinbeck forged for himself a type of social realism that transcends local barriers and places him with the great Russian novelists like Tolstoy, Dostoevsky and Gorky who raised novel to the status of the epic by depicting contemporary social reality on a gigantic scale. Steinbeck's deep concern for the social upheavals of his times, as shown in his novels like *The Grapes of Wrath*, gives him the status of a reformer. His concern for common human values like compassion, love and understanding makes him a humanist. His realism is not as depressing as were the social realities of the time he lived in. While the contemporary literature wallowed in despondency and skepticism, Steinbeck maintained a sturdy faith in abiding human values. Unlike his contemporaries, he inducted in his realism a hopeful and optimistic spirit. As Alfred Kazin observes:

> Steinbeck, standing apart from both the contemporary naturalists and the new novel of sensibility that one finds in Faulkner and Wolfe, brought a fresh note into contemporary fiction because he promised a realism less

> terror-ridden than the depression novel, yet one consciously responsible to society; a realism mindful of the terror and disorganization of contemporary life, but not submissive to the spiritual stupor of the times; a realism equal in some measure, if only in its aspiration, to the humanity, the gaiety, the wholeness, of realism in a more stable period.[25]

Whereas the depression novelists, according to Kazin, saw life as one "vast Chicago slaughterhouse, a guerrilla war, a perpetual bombing raid," Steinbeck showed a refreshing belief in human fellowship and courage. His humanism makes him accept the rhythm of life. Unlike Emile Zola's Steinbeck's realism is of a constructive nature; it is affirmative in tone. As Dr. K. Sreenivasan puts it: "Steinbeck's realism is satisfying because it provides illumination and delight. It is affirmative in nature and induces acceptance of life. Never does it sponsor defeatism. This is a trait which he shares with the great masters of European Fiction."[26] His is a creative realism which is evident in theme, characterization, setting and style. He is basically a humanist and his faith in man remains unswerving.

Geographical setting and the socio-cultural background always play an important part in a writer's selection of his themes. Steinbeck is no exception to the rule. The greatest single influence on John Steinbeck's life and work was his Californian origin. Coming from the extreme South West coast of the United States, Steinbeck's favourite region in this area was the Salinas Valley, a geographical setting of most of his novels. He had grown up and matured with the woods, the creatures, the landscapes, the people of the valley. The growing Steinbeck had loved outdoor life and manual labour. As a student of Stanford University, he had worked at odd jobs like a rancher, a road worker, a deck hand, a cotton picker, etc. He was always comfortable, rather more at ease in the company of the affluent. Steinbeck's commitment as a writer to the lower strata of society makes sense when seen in the light of this geographical, social and cultural background. Himself coming from an enlightened and cultured domestic background, Steinbeck inherited a strong sense of justice and fairplay which, after his contact with the underdogs around, grew into a deep, lasting bond of sympathy, even empathy, making him the writer that he is. As Thomas Kiernan remarks: "The characters who populate his work, the exterior landscapes and the interior settings in which the action of his stories occurs, as well as the description and imagery he uses to chart and define his characters and places—almost invariably are derived from his younger years."[27] Steinbeck's deep involvement with the life of his native valley gives him a stamp of authority and he gives a convincing report of the life-cycles of the gardeners, mystics, adventurers and the like.

Being more conversant with the life of the poor than with the life of the rich, Steinbeck gives us the inside view of the lives of the lower strata of society. He invariably chooses to relate the day-to-day experiences of the ordinary human beings. He takes up those aspects of their lives as themes of his novels which have a universal appeal. For instance, the theme of loneliness and alienation in *Cup of Gold*, of exploitation of the poor by the rich in his novels of the 30s, of degeneration of human values in the materialistic society in *The Winter of Our Discontent are* all treated in a manner that it is not the political struggle nor the economic strife between the two classes but their human feelings of love and hatred, their human qualities of suffering and endurance, etc., which are made central to the reader's experience. Steinbeck's realism helps him portray American life in its vividness. He is rightly acclaimed in his Nobel Prize citation "as an independent expounder of the truth with an unbiased instinct for what is genuinely American, be it good or wicked."[28]

Thus, Steinbeck holds in the history of American novel the middle place between the cultural stream of the New England origin nourished by giant figures like Hawthorne, James and Hemingway and the regional stream of the Southern origin carried on by Twain, Faulkner and O'Conner. His middle position, marked by the socio-economic concern, comes closer to the English and European traditions of the novel than does either the cultural tradition of the North or the regional tradition of the South. As one of the major figures of this larger tradition than the mere American, Steinbeck always remains a representative novelist of America between the two World Wars. Notwithstanding his limitations as creator of women in his fiction, his treatment of women in the historical context of his time is unmatched by any other novelist of the time. His women may not be heroic like Hester Pryne, archetypal like Isabel Archer, representative of the New Women like Brett Ashley, but they are certainly closer to the real women they are meant to represent in the American society between the two Wars. Besides, these women figures are more representative of the common mass of the female kind who embody, not a philosophy, myth, or phenomenon, but the real complex of human emotions for which women have always been known. Thus, Steinbeck is both more truly American as well as more truly universal than novelists like Hawthorne, James and Hemingway in his characterization of women as well as otherwise.

Notes

1 William H. Chafe, *The American Women: Her Changing Social, Economic and Political Roles 1920-1970* (New York: Oxford University Press, 1972)25.

2 Barbara J. Harris, *Beyond Her Sphere: Women and the Professions in American History* (London, England: Greenwood Press, 1978) 134.

3 Susan Ware, *Holding Their Own: American Women in the 1930s* (Boston: Twayne Publishers, 1982)66.

4 *Ibid.*, 10-11.

5 Barbara J.Harris, *Beyond Her Sphere* (1978) 141-142.

6 Susan Ware, *Holding Their Own* (1982) 27.

7 *Ibid.*

8 *Ibid.*, 1.

9 *The Grapes of Wrath*, 577.

10 Susan Ware, *Holding Their Own* (1982) 184.

11 William H. Chafe, *The American Women* (1972) 146.

12 Ernest R. Groves, *The American Women: The Feminine Side of a Masculine Civilization* (New York: Arno Press, 1972) 370-71.

13 Susan M. Hartmann, *The Home Front and Beyond: American Women in the 1940s* (Boston: Twayne Publishers, 1982) 23.

14 William H. Chafe, *The American Women* (1972) 176.

15 Barbara J. Harris, *Beyond Her Sphere* (1978) 165.

16 Susan M. Hartmann, ***The Home Front and Beyond*** (1982) 114.

17 *Ibid.*, 201.

18 Barbara J. Harris, *Beyond Her Sphere* (1978) 165.

19 Mary Mchugh, *The Women Thing* (New York: Praeger Publishers, 1973) 27.

20 *Ibid.*, 20.

21 G.B. Shaw, *"Preface"* Mrs. Warren's Profession in Seven Plays (New York: Dodd, Mead and Co., 1951) 3.

22 Robert E. Morsberger, "Steinbeck's Happy Hookers," *Steinbeck's Women: Essays in Criticism* (1979) 39.

23 Susan Ware, *Holding Their Own* (1982) 60.

24 *Ibid.*, 8.

25 Alfred Kazin, *On Native Grounds* (1942) 393-94.

26 Dr. K. Sreenivasan, *John Steinbeck: A Study of His Novels* (1980) 181.

27 Thomas Kiernan, *The Intricate Music: A Biography of John Steinbeck* (Boston: Little, Brown And Company, 1979) 19.

28 *The New York Times* Oct. 27 (1962) 12.

Bibliography

Primary Sources

Steinbeck, John. *Cup of Gold.* Cleveland and New York: The World Publishing Company, 1944. First Published in 1929.

——. *The Pastures of Heaven.* London: Quality Press Limited, 1953. First published in 1932.

——. *To a God Unknown. London:* Transworld Publishers Ltd., 1973. First Published in 1933.

——. *Tortilla Flat.* New York: The Viking Press, 1947. First Published in 1935.

——. *In Dubious Battle.* New York: The Modern Library, 1936. First Published in 1936.

——. *Of Mice and Men.* From *The Short Novels of John Steinbeck.* New York: The Viking Press, 1953. First Published in 1937.

——. *The Red Pony.* New York : The Viking press, 1945. First Published in 1937.

——. *The Long Valley.* New York : The Viking Press, 1963. First Published in 1938.

——. *The Grapes of Wrath.* New York: The Viking Press, 1958. First Published in 1939.

——. *The Moon Is Down.* New York: The Viking Press, 1942.

——.*The Portable Steinbeck*. New York: The Viking Press, 1962. First Published in 1943.

——.*Cannery Row*. From *The Short Novels of Steinbeck*. New York: The Viking Press, 1953. First Published in 1945.

——.*The Wayward Bus*. New York: The Viking Press, 1947.

——.*The Pearl*. New York: The Viking Press, 1947.

——.*Burning Bright*. Great Britain: William Heinemann Ltd., 1951. First Published in 1950.

——.*East of Eden*. London: Pan Books Ltd., 1970. First Published in 1952.

——.*Sweet Thursday*. New York: The Viking Press, 1954.

——.*The Short Reign of Pippin IV*. New York: The Viking Press, 1957.

——.*The Winter of Our Discontent*. New York: The Viking Press, 1961.

Non-Fiction

——.*The Forgotten Village*. New York: The Viking Press, 1941.

——.*Sea of Cortez*. New York: The Viking Press, 1941.

——.*Bombs Away*. New York: The Viking Press, 1942.

——.*A Russian Journal*. New York: The Viking Press, 1948.

——.*The Log from the Sea of Cortez*. New York: The Viking Press, 1951.

——.*Once There Was a War*. London : Heinemann, 1959. First Published in 1958.

——.*Travels With Charley in Search of America*. New York: The Viking Press, 1962.

——.*America and Americans*. London: Heinemann, 1966.

——.*Journal of a Novel; The East of Eden Letters*. New York: The Viking Press, 1969.

——.*In Touch*. New York: Dell, 1969.

——.*Viva Zapata*. New York: The Viking Press, 1975.

Articles

——.Critics, Critics Burning Bright." *Saturday Review of Literature* XXXIII. Nov. 11 (1950): 20-21.

—–."My Short Novels." *English Journal* XLIII (1954): 147.

—–."Autobiography: Making of A New Yorker." *New York Times Magazine* Sept. 1955.

—–."A Letter on Criticism." *Colorado Quarterly* Autumn 1955.

—–."Critics—from a Writer's Viewpoint." *Saturday Review* XXXVIII. Aug. 1955: 20 & 28.

—–."*A Primer on the Thirties.*" *Esquire* 80. 4, Oct. 1973.

Secondary Sources

Alexander, Stanley. "*Cannery Row* : Steinbeck's Pastoral Poem." *Western American Literature* 2 (1968): 281-98.

—–."The Conflict of Form in *Tortilla Flat.*" *American Literature* 40 (1968): 58-66.

Alexander, Stanley Gerald. *Primitivism and Pastoral Form in John Steinbeck's Early Fiction.* Ann Arbor, Michigan: University of Microfilms, 1965.

Allen, Walter. *Tradition and Dream: The English and American Novel.* London: Phoenix House, 1965.

Andrew, Joe. *Women in Russian Literature 1780-1863.* London: The Macmillan Press Ltd., 1988.

Antico, John. "A Reading of Steinbeck's "'Flight.'" *Modern Fiction Studies* XI. Spring (1965): 45-53.

Astro, Richard, and Tetsumaro Hayashi, eds. *Steinbeck: The Man and His Work.* Corvallis: Oregon State University Press, 1971.

—–.*John Steinbeck and Edward F. Ricketts: The Shaping of a Novelist.* Minneapolis: The University of Minnesota Press, 1973.

Baker, Carlos. "*In Dubious Battle* Revalued." *New York Times Book Review* 25 July 1943: 5 & 16.

Beach, Joseph Warren. *American Fiction: 1920-1940.* New York: The Macmillan Company. 1941.

—–." John Steinbeck: The Journeyman Artist." *Steinbeck And His Critics.* Eds. E.W. Tedlock and C.V. Wicker. Albuquerque: The University of New Mexico Press, 1957.

Beach, Joseph Warren. "Taken All Together." *John Steinbeck: A Study of the Short Fiction.* By R.S. Hughes. Boston: Twayne Publishers, 1989.

Beatty, Sandra. "A Study of Female Characterization in Steinbeck's Fiction." *Steinbeck's Women: Essays in Criticism.* Ed. Tetsumaro Hayashi. Muncie, Indiana: Ball State University, 1979.

——."Steinbeck's Play-Women: A Study of the Female Presence in *Of Mice and Men, Burning Bright, The Moon Is Down, and Viva Zapata!" Steinbeck's Women: Essays in Criticism.* Ed. Tetsumaro Hayashi, Muncie. Indiana: Ball State University, 1979.

Beebe, Maurice, and Jackson R. Bryer. "Criticism of John Steinbeck: A Selected Checklist." *Modern Fiction Studies* XI. Spring (1965): 90-103.

Bennett, Robert. *The Wrath of John Steinbeck.* Los Angeles: The Albertson Press, 1939.

Benson, Jackson J. *The True Adventures of John Steinbeck.* New York: The Viking Press, 1984.

——.*Looking for Steinbeck's Ghost.* Norman And London: University of Oklahoma Press, 1988.

Bluefarb, Sam. *The Escape Motif In the American Novel.* U S A: Ohio State University Press, 1972.

Bowron, Bernard. "*The Grapes of Wrath*: A 'Wagons West' Romance." *Colorado Quarterly III* (1954): 84-91.

Bracher, Frederick. "Steinbeck and the Biological View of Man." *Pacific Spectator II.* Winter (1948): 14-29.

Brown, Daniel R. "A Monolith of Logic Against Waves of Nonsense." *Renascence* XVI (1963): 48-51.

Browning, Chris. "Grape Symbolism in *The Grapes of Wrath.*" Discourse 11 (1968): 129-40.

Burgum, Edwin B. "The Sensibility of John Steinbeck." *Science and Society.* Spring (1946): 132-147.

Calverton, V.F. "Steinbeck, Hemingway and Faulkner." *Modern Quarterly* XI. Fall 1939.

Cannon, Gerard, "The Pauline Apostleship of Tom Joad." *College English* XXIV (1962): 222-24.

Carlson, Eric W. "Symbolism in *The Grapes of Wrath.*" *College English* XIX (1958): 172-75.

Carpenter, Frederick I. "The Philosophical Joads." *College English* II. June 1941: 315-25.

——."John Steinbeck: American Dreamer." *Southwest Review* XXVI (1941): 454-67.

Chafe, William H. *The American Women; Her Changing Social, Economic and Political Roles 1920-1970.* New York: Oxford University Press, 1972.

Chametzky, Jules. "The Ambivalent Endings of *The Grapes of Wrath.*" *Modern Fiction Studies* XI. Spring (1965): 33-45.

Champney, Freeman. "John Steinbeck: Californian." The Antioch Review VII 1947.

Cowley, Malcom. "A Farewell to the 1930s" in Agnes McNeill Donohue, ed. *A Casebook On The Grapes of Wrath.* New York: Crowell, 1968.

Crockett, H. Kelly. "The Bible and *The Grapes of Wrath.*" College English XXIV (1962): 193-199.

Davis, Robert Con., ed. *The Grapes of Wrath: A Collection of Critical Essays.* Englewood Cliffs, N.J. : Prentice Hall, Inc., 1982.

——.Introduction. *The Grapes of Wrath: A Collection of Critical Essays.* Englewood Cliffs, N.J.: Prentice-Hall, Inc., 1982.

Davis, Robert Murray, ed. *Steinbeck: A Collection of Critical Essays.* Englewood Cliffs, N.J.: Prentice-Hall, Inc., 1972.

——.Introduction. *Steinbeck: A Collection of Critical Essays.* Ed. Robert Murray Davis. Englewood Cliffs, N.J.: Prentice-Hall, inc., 1972.

Demott, Robert. "Cathy Ames and Lady Godiva: A contribution to *East of Eden's* Background." *Steinbeck Quarterly* 1981.

De Schweinitz, George. "Steinbeck and Christianity." *College English* XIX (1958): 369.

Ditsky, John. "Land Nostalgia in the Novels of Faulkner, Cather, and Steinbeck." *Dissertation Abstracts International* 28 (1967): 1072A.

——.*Essays on East of Eden.* Muncie, Indiana: Ball State University, 1977. (Steinbeck Monograph Series, No.7).

——.*John Steinbeck: Life, Work, And Criticism.* Canada: York Press Ltd., 1985.

——."Steinbeck's "European" Play-Novella: *The Moon Is Down." Steinbeck Quarterly* Vol. XV. 1-2 Winter-Spring, 3-4 Summer-Fall, 1987.

Ditsky, John. *Critical Essays on Steinbeck's The Grapes of Wrath.* Boston, Massachusetts: G.K. Hall & Co., 1989.

Donohue, Agnes McNeill. "The Endless Journey to No End: Journey and Eden Symbolism in Hawthorne and Steinbeck." *A Casebook On The Grapes of Wrath.* New York: Crowell, 1968.

——,ed. *A Casebook On The Grapes of Wrath.* New York: Thomas Y. Crowell Company, 1970 (First Published in 1968).

Dougherty, Charles T. "The Christ-Figure in *The Grapes of Wrath." College English* XXIV (1962): 224-26.

Eisinger, Chester E. "Jeffersonian Agrarianism in *The Grapes of Wrath." University Kansas City Review* XIV (1947): 149-54.

Erikson, Erik H. "Inner and Outer Space: Reflections on Womenhood." From *The Women in America.* Boston: Houghton Mifflin Company, 1965.

Everest, Beth and Judy Weddles. "The Neglected Rib: Women in *East of Eden." Steinbeck Quarterly* Vol. XXI. No. 1-2 Winter-Spring 1988.

Fairley, Barker. "John Steinbeck and the Coming Literature." *Sewanee Review* 50. April-June 1942.

Fensch, Thomas. *Steinbeck and Covici: The Story of a Friendship.* Middlebury, Vermont: Paul S. Eriksson, 1979.

——,ed. *Conversations With John Steinbeck.* Jackson: University Press of Mississippi, 1988.

Ferrell, Keith. *John Steinbeck: The Voice of the Land.* New York: M. Evans and Company, Inc., 1986.

Fontenrose, Joseph. *John Steinbeck: An Introduction And Interpretation.* New York: Holt, Rinehart And Winston, Inc., 1963.

French, Warren. "Another Look at *The Grapes of Wrath." Colorado Quarterly* III (1955): 337-43.

——,*John Steinbeck.* 2nd ed. Boston: Twayne, 1975. First Print in 1961.

——,ed. *A Companion to The Grapes of Wrath.* New York: The Viking Press, 1964. First Published in 1963.

——, "Steinbeck's Winter Tale." *Modern Fiction Studies* XI. Spring (1965): 66-74.

——. *The Social Novel at the End of Era.* Carbondale: Southern Illinois University Press, 1966.

——, ed. *The Thirties: Fiction, poetry, Drama.* Deland, Fla: Everett Edwards, Inc., 1967.

——. "John Steinbeck." *Fifteen Modern American Authors: A Survey of Research and Criticism.* Ed. Jackson R. Bryer. Durham, N.C: Duke University Press, 1969.

——, ed. *The Fifties: Fiction, Poetry, Drama.* Deland, Fla: Everett Edwards, 1970.

——, "A Turning Point in Steinbeck Studies." Introduction. *The Novels of John Steinbeck: A Critical Study.* Columbia, Missouri: University of Missouri Press, 1974.

Frolock, W.M. "John Steinbeck's Men of Wrath." *Southwest Review* XXI (1946): 144-152.

Ganapathy R. "Steinbeck's *Of Mice and Men*: A Study of Lyricism Through Primitivism." *Literary Criterion* V. iii (1962): 101-104.

Gannet, Lewis. *John Steinbeck: Personal and Bibliographical Notes.* New York: The Viking Press, 1939.

——, "John Steinbeck's Way of Writing." Introduction. *The Portable Steinbeck.* New York: The Viking Press, 1962. First Published in 1943.

Garcia, Reloy. "Steinbeck's 'The Snake': An Explication." *Steinbeck Quarterly* Vol. V. 3-4, Summer-Fall 1972.

——, *Steinbeck and D.H. Lawrence: Fictive Voices and the Ethical Imperatives.* Muncie, Indiana: Ball State University, 1972. (Steinbeck Monograph Series, No.2).

Geismer, Maxwell. *Writers in Crisis: The American Novel Between Two Wars.* Boston: Houghton, 1942.

——, "Fable Retold." *Saturday Review of Literature* 30. 20 Nov. 1947.

——, *American Moderns: From Rebellion to Conformity.* New York: Hill and Wang, 1958.

Gerstenberger, Donna. "Steinbeck's American Waste Land." *Modern Fiction Studies* XI. Spring (1965): 59-65.

Gibbs, Lincoln R. "John Steinbeck: Moralist." *The Antioch Review* June 1942.

Gladstein, Mimi Reisel. "Female Characters in Steinbeck: Minor Characters of Major Importance." *Steinbeck's Women: Essays in Criticism.* Ed. Tetsumaro Hayashi. Muncie, Indiana: Ball State University, 1979.

Gladstein, Mimi Reisel. "Steinbeck's Juana: A Women of Worth." *Steinbeck's Women: Essays in Criticism.* Ed. Tetsumaro Hayashi. Muncie, Indiana: Ball State University, 1979.

—,"Ma Joad and Pilar: Significantly Similar." *Steinbeck Quarterly* 1981.

—,*The Indestructible Women in Faulkner, Hemingway, and Steinbeck.* Michigan, Ann Arbor: UMI Research Press, 1986.

Glazier, Lyle. *Decadence and Rebirth: Hacettepe Lectures in American Literature.* Ankara: Hacettepe University Publishers, 1971.

Goldsmith, Arnold L. "Thematic Rhythm in *The Red Pony.*" *College English* XXVI (1965): 391-394.

Golemba, Henry L. "Steinbeck's Attempt to Escape the Literary Fallacy." *Modern Fiction Studies* Vol. 15. 2-4 Winter 1969-70.

Gray, James. *John Steinbeck.* Minneapolis: University of Minnesota Press, 1971.

Griffin, Robert J., and William A. Freedman. "Machines and Animals: Pervasive Motifs in *The Grapes of Wrath.*" *Journal of English and Germanic Philosophy* LXII (1963): 569-80.

Gurko, Leo. "From the Angry Decade." *The Angry Decade.* 1947. rpt. in Agnes McNeill Donohue, ed. *A Casebook On The Grapes of Wrath.* New York: Crowell, 1968.

Hartmann, Susan M. *The Home Front and Beyond: American Women in the 1940s.* Boston: Twayne Publishers, 1982.

Hayashi, Tetsumaro. Women and the Principle of Continuity in *The Grapes of Wrath.*" *Kyushu American Literature* 10 (1967): 75-80.

Hayashi, Tetsumaro. "Steinbeck's Women in *The Grapes of Wrath*: A New Perspective." *Kyushu American Literature* 18. 1-4, 1967.

——. *John Steinbeck: A Concise Bibliography*. Metuchen, N.J.: Scarecrow, 1967.

——. ed. *Steinbeck's Literary Dimension: A Guide to Comparative Studies*. Metuchen, N.J.: The Scarecrow Press, Inc., 1973.

——. ed. *A Study Guide to Steinbeck: A Handbook to His Major Works*. Metuchen, N.J.: The Scarecrow Press, Inc., 1974.

Hayashi, Tetsumaro, Yasuo Hashiguchi, and Richard F. Peterson, eds. *John Steinbeck: East and West*. Muncie, Indiana: Ball State University, 1978. (Steinbeck Monograph Series, No.8).

Hayashi, Tetsumaro, ed. *Steinbeck's Women: Essays in Criticism*. Muncie, Indiana: Ball State University, 1979. (Steinbeck Monograph Series, No. 9).

— ,ed. *Steinbeck's Travel Literature: Essays in Criticism*. Muncie, Indiana: Ball State University, 1980. (Steinbeck Monograph Series, No. 10).

Hoffman, Frederick J. *The Modern Novel in America 1900-1950*. Chicago: Henry Regnery Company, 1951.

Holman, Hugh. "A Narrow-Gauge Dickens."*New Republic* CXXX. June 7 (1954): 18-20.

Hughes, R.S. *Beyond 'The Red Pony': A Reader's Companion to Steinbeck's Complete Short Stories*. Metuchen, N.J., & London: The Scarecrow Press, Inc., 1987.

Hughes, R.S. *John Steinbeck: A Study of the Short Fiction*. Boston: Twayne Publishers, 1989.

Hyman, Stanley Edgar. "Some Notes on John Steinbeck." *The Antioch Review* 2 Summer 1942.

Isherwood, Christopher. "The Tragedy of Eldorado." *Kenyon Review* 1939. rpt. in Agnes McNeill Donohue, ed. *A Casebook On The Grapes of Wrath*. New York: Crowell, 1968.

J. Harris, Barbara. *Beyond Her Sphere: Women and the Professions in American History*. Westport, Connecticutt: Greenwood Press, 1978.

Jackson, Joseph Henry. "John Steinbeck: A Portrait." *Saturday Review* Vol. 1. No. 22, Sept. 25, 1937.

——. Introduction. *The Short Novels of John Steinbeck*. New York: The Viking Press, 1953.

Jain, Sunita. *John Steinbeck's Concept of Man: A Critical Study of His Novels.* New Delhi: New Statesman, 1979.

Johnson, Curtis L. "Steinbeck: A Suggestion for Research." *Modern Fiction Studies* XI. i Spring (1965): 75-78.

Jones, Claude E. "Proletarian Writing and John Steinbeck." *Sewanee Review* XLVIII (1940): 445-56.

Jones, Lawrence William. *John Steinbeck as Fabulist.* Muncie, Indiana: Ball State University, 1973. (Steinbeck Monograph Series, No.3).

Jones, William M. "Steinbeck's 'Flight.' " *Explicator* XVIII 1959.

Kallapur, S.T. "John Steinbeck and Oriental Thought: Some Parallels." *The Image of India in Western Creative Writing*. Madras: Macmillan and Company, 1971.

Karsten, Ernest E., Jr. "Thematic Structure in *The Pearl.*" *English Journal* LIV (1965): 1-7.

Kazin, Alfred. *On Native Grounds: An Interpretation of Modern American Prose Literature.* New York: Reynal and Hitchcock, 1942.

Kennedy, John S. "John Steinbeck: Life Affirmed and Dissolved." *Fifty Years of the American Novel.* New York: Charles Scribner's Sons, 1951.

Kiernan, Thomas. *The Intricate Music: A Biography of John Steinbeck*. Boston: Little, Brown And Company, 1979.

Kinney, Arthur F. "The Arthurian Cycle in *Tortilla Flat.*" *Modern Fiction Studies* XI. i spring (1965): 11-20.

Krutch, Joseph Wood. "John Steinbeck's Dramatic Tale of Three Generations." *The New York Herald Tribune Book Review* Sept. 21, 1955.

Langford, Richard E., ed. *Essays in Modern American Literature.* Deland, Fla: Stetson University Press, 1963, 76-89.

Leonard, Frank G. "Cozzens Without Sex; Steinbeck Without Sin." *The Antioch Review* XVIII. No.2, Summer (1958): 209-18.

Levant, Howard. *The Novels of John Steinbeck: A Critical Study.* Columbia, Missouri: University of Missouri Press, 1974.

——."The Unity of In *Dubious Battle*: Violence and Dehumanization." *Modern Fiction Studies* XI. i Spring (1965): 21-33.

Levenson, Samuel. "The Compassion of John Steinbeck." *Canadian Forum* XX Sept. 1940.

Levidova. "The Post-War Books of John Steinbeck." *Soviet Review* Vol. 4 No.2, Summer 1963.

Lewis, R.W.B. "John Steinbeck: The Fitful Daemon." *The Young Rebel in American Literature*. Ed. Carl Bode. London: William Heinemann, 1959.

Lifton, Robert J., ed. *The Women in America*. Boston: Houghton Mifflin Company, 1965.

Lisca, Peter. "Motif and Pattern in *Of Mice and Men*." Modern Fiction Studies 11 (1956): 228-234.

———."The Art of John Steinbeck: An Analysis and Interpretation of Its Development." *Dissertation Abstracts International* XVI (1956): 965.

———."John Steinbeck: A Literary Biography." *Steinbeck and His Critics*. Albuquerque: *The University of New Mexico Press, 1957.*

———. "*The Grapes of Wrath* as Fiction." *Publications of the Mod. Lang. Assn. of America* LXXII (1957): 296-309.

———.*The Wide World of John Steinbeck*. Brunswick, New Jersey: Rutgers University Press, 1958.

———."Steinbeck's Image of Man and His Decline as a Writer." *Modern Fiction Studies* XI.i Spring (1965): 3-10.

———."Steinbeck and Hemingway." *Steinbeck Newsletter* Spring 1969. Span Dec. 1969.

Lisca, Peter. *John Steinbeck: Nature and Myth*. New York: Thomas Y. Crowell Company, 1978.

Magny, Claude Edmonde. "*East of Eden.*" *Perspective* USA V(1953): 146-52.

Marcus, Mordecai. "The Lost Dream of Sex and Childbirth in 'The Chrysanthemums.' " *Modern Fiction Studies* XI. i Spring (1965): 54-58.

Marks, Lester Jay. *Thematic Designs In the Novels of John Steinbeck*. Paris, The Hague: Mouton and Co., Printers, 1969.

Martin, Stoddard. *California Writers: Jack London, John Steinbeck, the tough guys*. London: Macmillan, 1983.

Matsumoto, Fusae. "Steinbeck's Women in *The Long Valley*." *John Steinbeck East and West*. Eds. Yasuo Hashiguchi and Richard F. Peterson. Muncie,

Indiana: Ball State University, 1978. (Steinbeck Monograph Series, No.8).

May, Charles E. "Myth and Mystery in Steinbeck's 'The Snake': A Jungian View." *John Steinbeck: A Study of Short Fiction*. R.S. Hughes. Boston: Twayne Publishers, 1989.

McCarthy, Paul. *John Steinbeck*. New York: Frederic Ungar Publishing Co., 1980.

Mchugh, Mary. *The Women Thing*. New York: Praeger Publishers, 1973.

McMahan, Elizabeth E. " 'The Chrysanthemums': Study of a Women's Sexuality." *Modern Fiction Studies* Vol. 14. No.4, Winter 1968.

McWilliams, Carey. "California Pastoral." *Antioch Review* 1942. rpt. in Agnes McNeill Donohue, ed. *A Casebook On The Grapes of Wrath*. New York: Crowell, 1968.

Metzger, Charles R. "Steinbeck's Version of the Pastoral." *Modern Fiction Studies* VI Summer (1960): 115-24.

Miller, William V. "Sexual and Spiritual Ambiguity in 'The Chrysanthemums.'" *Steinbeck Quarterly* Vol. V. Summer-Fall 1972.

Mitchell, Marilyn L. "Steinbeck's Strong Women: Feminine identity in the Short Stories." *Southwest Review* 64. 1976.

Mizener, Arthur. "Does a Moral Vision of the Thirties Deserve a Nobel Prize?" *The New York Times Book Review* Dec. 9, 1962.

Moloney, Michael F. "Half-Faiths in Modern Fiction." *Catholic World* CLXXI. Aug. 1950.

Moore, Harry Thornton. *The Novels of John Steinbeck: A First Critical Study*. Chicago: Normandie House, 1939.

Moore, Ward. "Cannery Row Revisited: Steinbeck and Sardine." *Nation* CLXXIX. Oct. 16 (1954): 325-27.

Morris, Harry. "*The Pearl*: Realism and Allegory." *English Journal* LII (1963): 487-95 and 505.

Morsberger, Robert E. "Steinbeck's Happy Hookers." *Steinbeck's Women: Essays in Criticism.* Ed. Tetsumaro Hayashi. Muncie, Indiana: Ball State University, 1979.

Motley, Warren. "From Patriarchy to Matriarchy: Ma Joad's Role in *The*

Grapes of Wrath." American Literature 54. Oct.3, 1982.

Nakashima, Saikichi. "Steinbeck's Women: A Synopsis of the Reports of the Annual Seminar." *Kyushu American Literature* 1975.

Nelson, Harland S. "Steinbeck's Politics Then and Now." *Antioch Review* 27 (1967): 118-33.

Nevius Blake. "Steinbeck: One Aspect." *The Pacific Spectator* III. Summer (1949): 302-310.

Nicholas, Lewis "Talk With John Steinbeck." *New York Times Book Review* 30. Sept. 28, 1952.

O'Connor, Richard. *John Steinbeck*. New York: McGraw-Hill Book Company, 1970.

Osbrone, William R. "The Texts of Steinbeck's 'The Chrysanthemums.'" *Modern Fiction Studies* 12. No. 4 Winter (1966): 479-84.

Owens, Louis D. "Steinbeck's 'The Murder': Illusions of Chivalry." *Steinbeck Quarterly* 1985.

——.*John Steinbeck's Re-Vision of America*. Athens: The University of Georgia Press, 1985.

——."Winter in Paris: John Steinbeck's Pippin IV." *Steinbeck Quarterly* Vol. XV, 1987.

——.The Grapes of Wrath: *Trouble in the Promised Land*. Boston: Twayne Publishers, 1989.

Pellow, C. Kenneth. " 'The Chrysanthemums' Revisited." *Steinbeck Quarterly* Vol. XXII. No. 1-2, Winter-Spring 1989.

Phillips, William. "Male-ism and Moral-ism." *American Mercury* LXXV (1953): 93-98.

Pierre, Brian St. *John Steinbeck: The California Years*. San Francisco: Chronicle Books, 1983.

Pollock, Theodore. "On the Ending of *The Grapes of Wrath." Modern Fiction Studies* IV (1958): 177-78.

Poore, Charles. Introduction. *The Grapes of Wrath*. New York: Harper, 1951.

Powell, Lawrence Clark. Foreward. *The Wrath of John Steinbeck*. Los Angeles: The Albertson Press, 1939.

Pratt, John Clark. *John Steinbeck: A Critical Essay.* Grand Rapids, Michigan: William B. Eerdmans Publisher, 1970.

R. Groves, Ernest. *The American Women: The Feminine Side of a Masculine Civilization.* New York: Arno Press, 1972.

Rao, B. Ramachandra. *The American Fictional Hero.* New Delhi: Babri Publications Private Ltd., 1979.

Rasco, Burton. "John Steinbeck." *The English Journal* March 1938.

Renner, Stanley. "Sexual Idealism and Violence in 'The White Quail.'" *Steinbeck Quarterly* 1984.

——."Mary Teller and Sue Bridehead: Birds of a Feather in '*The White Quail*' *and Jude the Obscure.*" *Steinbeck Quarterly* 1985.

Richard, Edmund C. "The Challenge of John Steinbeck." *The North American Review* Vol. 2 and 3. No.2, Summer 1937.

Ross, Woodburn. "John Steinbeck: Earth and Stars." *Studies in Honor of A.H.R. Fairchild.* Ed. by Charles T. Prouty. Columbia: University of Missouri Press, 1946.

——."John Steinbeck: Naturalism's Priest." *College English* X May (1949): 432-37.

Sands, Maurice. *An Outline of Modern American Novel.* Boston, Mass: Student Outlines Company, 1946.

Satyanarayan, M.R. "John Steinbeck's *The Winter of Our Discontent*: A New Phase." *Osmania Journal of English Studies* 6. 1, 1967.

Satyanarayan, M.R. *John Steinbeck: A Study of the Theme of Compassion.* Hyderabad: Vidyarthi Publications, 1977.

Schulberg, Budd. *The Four Seasons of Success.* Garden City, New York: Doubleday, 1972.

Seixas, Antonia. "John Steinbeck and The Teleological Bus." *Game and Gossip* Vol. 1. No. 12, March 1947.

Sharma, R.K., ed. *Indian Responses to Steinbeck.* Jaipur: Rachna Prakashan, 1984.

Shockley, Martin S. "The Reception of *The Grapes of Wrath* in Oklahoma." *American Literature* XV. (1944): 351-61.

——."Christian Symbolism in *The Grapes of Wrath.*" *College English* XVIII (1956): 87-90.

Simmonds, Roy S. *Steinbeck's Literary Achievement*. Muncie, Indiana: Ball State University, 1976. (Steinbeck Monograph Series, No.6).

——."Steinbeck and World War II: The Moon Goes Down." *Steinbeck Quarterly* 1984.

——."Cathy Ames and Rhoda Penmark: Two Child Monsters." *Mississippi Quarterly* Vol. 39. 2 Spring 1986.

Snell, George D. *The Shapers of American Fiction*. New York: Dutton, 1947.

Simpson, Arthur L., Jr. " 'The White Quail': A Portrait of An Artist." *Steinbeck Quarterly* Vol. V. No. 3-4, Summer-Fall, 1972.

Spilka, Mark. "Of George and Lennie and Curley's Wife: Sweet Violence in Steinbeck's Eden." *Modern Fiction Studies* Vol. 20. No.2, Summer 1974.

Sreenivasan, Dr. K. *John Steinbeck: A Study of His Novels*. Trivendrum: College Book House, 1980.

Steinbeck, Elaine and Robert Wallasten, eds. *Steinbeck: A Life in Letters*. New York: The Viking Press, 1975.

Tarr, E. Whitney. "Steinbeck On One Plane." *Saturday Review of Literature* XXX. 20, 1947.

Taylor, Frank J. "California's *Grapes of Wrath*." *Forum* II, 1939. rpt. in Agnes McNeill Donohue, ed. *A Casebook on The Grapes of Wrath*. New York: Crowell, 1968.

Taylor, Walter Fuller. "*The Grapes of Wrath* Reconsidered." *Mississippi Quarterly* XII (1959): 136-44.

Tedlock, E.W., Jr. and C.V. Wicker. Introduction. *Steinbeck And His Critics*. Albuquerque: The University of New Mexico Press, 1957.

Tedlock, E.W., Jr. and C.V. Wicker, eds. *Steinbeck And His Critics: A Record of Twenty-Five Years*. Albuquerque: The University of New Mexico Press, 1957.

Timmerman, John H. *John Steinbeck's Fiction: The Aesthetics of the Road Taken*. Norman And London: University of Oklahoma Press, 1986.

Tuttleton, James W. "Steinbeck in Russia: The Rhetoric of Praise and Blame." *Modern Fiction Studies* XI. i Spring (1965): 79-89.

Uchida, Shigeharu. "John Steinbeck's Non-Teleology and *To a God Unknown*." *Kyushu American Literature* No.6 (1963): 13-17.

Uchida, Shigeharu. "Sentimental Steinbeck and His *Tortilla Flat.*" *Kyushu American Literature* No.7 (1964): 8-12.

Valjean, Nelson. *John Steinbeck: The Errant Knight*. San Francisco: Chronicle Books, 1975.

Vogel, Dan. "Steinbeck's 'Flight': The Myth of Manhood." *College English* XXIII (1961): 225-26.

Walcutt, Charles Child. *American Literary Naturalism: A Divided Stream.* Minneapolis: University of Minnesota Press, 1956.

Ware, Susan. *Holding Their Own: American Women in the 1930s.* Boston: Twayne Publishers, 1982.

Watt, F.W. *Steinbeck.* Edinburgh And London: Oliver And Boyd, 1962.

Weeks, Donald. "Steinbeck Against Steinbeck." *The Pacific Spectator* 1(1947): 447-57.

Whipple, T.K. "Steinbeck: Through a Glass. Though Brightly." *The New Republic* 96. Oct. 12, 1938.

——.*Study Out the Land.* Berkeley: University of California Press, 1943.

Williams, Merryn. *Women In the English Novel, 1800-1900.* London: Macmillan Press, 1985.

Wilson, Edmund. "The Californians: Storm and Steinbeck." *The New Republic* 103. Dec.9, 1940.

——."From Classics and Commercials." *Classics and Commercials.* rpt. in Agnes McNeill Donohue, ed. *A Casebook On The Grapes of Wrath.* New York: Crowell, 1968.

Woodress, James. "John Steinbeck: Hostage to Fortune." *Southern Atlantic Quarterly* LXIII 1964.

Wright, Celeste Turner. "Ancient Analogues of an Incident in John Steinbeck." *Western Folklore* XIV (1955): 50-51.